The Englishman's Handbook

by

Idries Shah

OTHER BOOKS BY IDRIES SHAH

The Englishman's Handbook:

or

How to
Deal with Foreigners

by

Idries Shah

THE OCTAGON PRESS
LONDON

ISBN 0 863040 77 2

First Published in 2000

Printed and bound in Great Britain by
Bookcraft (Bath) Ltd., Midsomer Norton, Somerset

Contents

Foreword

Who or what, exactly, is a foreigner? Annoyingly to the Brits, only non-British people are likely to ask this question. The English, you see, believe that they know the answer instinctively, feel it in their bones.

I think that they *have to* feel it in their bones, because the usages and definitions in this matter have been altered so often. This has happened from time to time and place to place, sometimes almost at a whim. And it is still happening.

For instance, how is a white, Anglo-Saxon 'incomer' from London to a Sussex village, not a hundred miles away seen locally? We have the full authority of the *Oxford English Dictionary* to state that such a person is, locally, called a foreigner. But a black boxer, born in the UK – especially if he's winning – will be referred to in media reports as 'the English boy'.

There is no other unchallenged, reliable way than instinct: so in-the-bones it has to be. And yet, in Britain, there is always a reason for what people do, as we shall see abundantly displayed in the course of this book. Foreigners who think otherwise simply have not done enough research. They are not always to be blamed for this. The investigations have to be conducted in unexpected places and by a highly sophisticated method. This latter includes reading and interpreting the meaning of news, feature and editorial items in English newspapers, as we shall see in due course.

But first, let us return to our original question: what is a foreigner? According to that venerable English reference work, *Haydn's Dictionary,* a foreigner is an alien. This word is, of course, itself of foreign, Latin, derivation: from *alius*, 'other'. But 'foreigner' is also a foreign word; it is of French ancestry, from *forein*, and thence from the Latin for 'out of doors'.

My own theory is that the English word for a foreigner has

3

changed as the English themselves have changed. Readers of my *Darkest England*[1], among others, will recall that the English were once — and for quite a long time — a wandering tribe. They were glimpsed now and then in such regions as Germania, east of the Elbe (by Tacitus) and by Ptolemy as dwelling near today's Magdeburg.

In their nomadic times, an outsider would, for them, have been someone outside the tribe or camp. Their old word, 'outlander', would, of course, not have sufficed in these fairly ancient times: since they had no land, they could hardly have seen anyone as 'out' of it.

When the Saxons settled farther west, in Schleswig, the outsiders would have been non-Schleswigians. These would, of course, have included the (Celtic and Romano-British) inhabitants of the British Isles.

When the English invaded Britain — a very short time ago in historical terms — they were themselves outlanders, foreigners, in the British Isles. For many centuries, they looked back towards their old home: rather like the colonial settlers of the British Empire. It is on record that the English of the British Isles referred to Schleswig as: 'Anglia Vetus' — old England.

Later, the English must have heard the word 'forein' applied to them by the Normans after the Conquest. After which, no doubt, they bemused the invaders by using it to describe *them*. This may well be the earliest example of the now widely-practised national custom of confusing people, especially foreigners, by adopting their customs.

For instance, in Saracen Spain, the noble descendants of the Prophet were the only people entitled to sport ostrich feathers in their helmets. Almost at once, English aristocrats took to this fashion, even if they had formerly been scurvy knaves without a single quartering to their shields. They took the hats from Russian soldiers, capes from Hungarians, swords from Mamlukes. All this helped to create the English — and later very British — Army.

'Stranger', the word in use before 'foreign', was also adopted from the French. They derived it from *extraneus* the Romans' word for extraneous, which means 'outside' or 'not essential'. This, incidentally, seems a very neat paraphrase of the English belief recorded by Lyly in 1580. He referred to:

'an olde saying, that all countries stand in neede of Britaine, and Britaine of none.'

There is, in fact, no purely English word in use today to signify a foreigner. The English have adopted other peoples' words.

But how about 'outlander'? It must be Saxon, surely . . . One authoritative source, *Chambers's Dictionary*, gives, among the meanings of Outlander, the definition 'uitlander'. But is that an English word? It sounded very Dutch to me, when I first found it; yet *Chambers's* refused to be more specific.

'Outlander, a foreigner; an uitlander' it insists.

But the *Oxford English Dictionary,* which bills itself as 'the supreme reference work on the English language' (in the strangely shrill, highly-undignified, un-British-sounding tone of the junk-mail advertisements constantly addressed to me), says it is indeed from The Netherlands. So, of course, it must be; though I still have to find an English person who is any the wiser when told that 'outlander' equals 'uitlander'.

It is as if you had said to an English person: 'the word for "house" is *maison*'. Why ever would you say that? Or who really wrote the entry in *Chambers's*? Were they employing a Dutch penny-a-liner whose definition (or conversation with a fellow Netherlander) slipped in unedited?

The English (and I don't blame them) tend to think that *I* must be from The Netherlands when I quote Dutch derivations cited by their own, British, standard dictionaries. Perhaps I reveal my own foreignness in asking why an English dictionary uses a foreign word to define another English word, especially one describing foreigners. Or perhaps *Chambers's* really was compiled for more erudite (and/or more Netherlandish) people than those whom I can find in England today.

Yet − although the word is not labelled obsolete or even rare by the OED − who has ever heard an English man, woman or child, speak of an 'outlander'? Let alone an 'uitlander'.

The OED, with the kind of general, gentle imprecision (not to mention barminess) with which one eventually and affectionately comes to associate it, avers that, although a foreigner comes from overseas:

In England the term [foreigner] is not commonly understood to include Americans.

The people of more than a score of nations, from the Arctic north to Mesoamerica and Patagonia in the opposite direction – Americans all – would surely be surprised to learn this. Especially, I suspect, if they had to deal with an Englishman – even one from the OED.

I have met many excellent but to me completely baffling Amerindians whose appearance, speech and habits I could swear have absolutely nothing in common with English people. Not understood as foreigners? Surely the pundits of the OED could not be making an elementary, semi-literate, mistake? Were they actually miscalling the citizens of the United States of [North] America 'the Americans'?

No, I could not believe that. Such a solecism might undermine – to put it no higher – the entire repute of the OED; and – Heaven forbid – even set people looking for other imperfections. No. They must mean ALL the Americans, of whatever complexion.

These people come from several racial stocks, arrived in the New World at widely different times, have several civilisations. They speak, it is thought, between one thousand and two thousand languages. These would surely defeat even the OED: they include French, English, Spanish, Portuguese and Guarani. Many Inuit, Mongolian, African, Sikh and Taiwanese immigrants in America, to mention but a few, are not, by this reckoning, foreigners to the English ... So they must be English.

I hope *they* don't mind.

I knew that Britain was the only country in the entire world which had citizens ('British Overseas Citizen') who were not allowed to enter the country of their nationality freely, if at all. But I never suspected that all the Americans – North, Central and South – were really English.

Many of the forbears of the people I have mentioned arrived in the Western Hemisphere long before the US citizens of European extraction. Thousands of years before, in fact. And thousands of years before the English arrived in England. Work that one out.

I'll give you a hint, you foreigners. It is an English characteristic to make a statement which sounds atrocious or improbable to a logical mind and then leave you to work out what it means.

Meanwhile, the Englishman has passed on to other things. Here is a small example:

One day I was lunching with an English war-leader, who had the reputation of having 'hit the enemy for six' in World War II, mostly by his masterful exploitation of terrain.

Expanding on his tactics in some battle or other, he waved his fork and declared, 'Let's face it, every country has a central plain.'

I was amazed. I had not personally conducted any especially victorious campaigns, but I *had* been in many countries with nary a central plain.

I could not restrain myself. Like a typical and insolent foreigner, I said: 'but, General, surely there are plenty of countries without central plains . . .'

He gave me a baleful look, and poured a glass of wine. After drinking it in one gulp, he muttered, 'Don't bother me with details', and went on with his narrative.

That is the English way. Can you, a foreigner, ever hope to match it? Of course not. Understand it? No.

Can you, the Englishman, better it? Certainly not. If you don't know it already, or if your expertise needs a little smartening up, your research material is everywhere, in England. Just talk to a few other people. I know that it is hard for a true-born Englishman to talk to strangers, but try. It will help you in dealing with foreignness: which, after all, is what much of this book is about.

Only the other day, the non-foreignness of Americans at least in one sense, was not readily perceptible to the head waiter at my London club; and he takes a lot of confusing. But, as you will see, he knew how to manage a tricky situation.

We have reciprocal hospitality arrangements with a United States 'gentlemen's club', and one of its Members, rather big in 'staaks'and 'baands', had just ordered something.

The head waiter sent a hurried note to our Librarian, to have the order translated. He had transcribed the thirsty transatlantic requirement phonetically as *'gimmi a baarrala minnal wohra'*.

He knew a foreign language when he heard it; and, luckily, our versatile Librarian had helped out in quite difficult situations of this kind in the past.

He, however, was also baffled and in the end a Canadian Member interpreted, though a trifle reluctantly.

He, it turned out, had 'suffered for years' from being mistaken for an American.

In the interests of research — and just to see what would happen — I informed the head waiter that an American, any American, according to the best authority, is not foreign at all.

'I do not, of course, doubt your assurances, Sir,' he answered. 'But I must continue to adhere to the view that Mr. Cyrus Z. Magillicuddy III's desire for a bottle of mineral water was itself couched in a foreign diction, which you will no doubt allow is not quite the same thing. Besides, I distinctly heard him claim to be of another nationality.'

'Indeed?' I could hardly believe my ears. An American, pretending to be something else?

'What did he say he was, then?'

'He said, "I was born a Statesider, I have lived a Statesider, and — Gaard willing — I'll die a Statesider. That's the nationality for me."'

English head waiters in the best clubs do tend to talk like the one in ours. Perhaps it is intended to confuse foreigners. However, our waiter was mollified by the Statesider-American's lack of rancour, and, indeed, his expression of hope that they would meet again the following day.

'He offered me a Confederate banknote (which I, of course, declined) and actually said "Seeya-amorra-fella,"' he beamed.

Now, I know quite a few Americans, especially the variety hailing from the gringo, not the Mexican, United States of (North) America. Unlike British Subjects trying to visit the USA, North Americans are often treated lightly by immigration officers when entering Britain. The greasers (Mexicans or Spanish-Americans, the dictionary says) are not treated as cordially as the Yanks. But the OED's 'common understanding' that Americans are not foreigners has not yet spread to the Aliens' Department of the Home Office in London.

Other countries have a Ministry of the Interior. Britain has, instead, The Home Office. Even British people are not at all sure what its responsibilities are. It does not really sound like a Ministry, or anything to do with police, immigration or foreigners. After all, there is a Foreign Office, although that has almost no foreigners in it.

One desperate foreigner whom I know, when told by an

immigration official to apply to the Home Office for permission to stay in the United Kingdom, looked up the words in a dictionary.

'Home' he read, meant 'habitual abode'. This seemed to mean that he should apply where he lived. As for 'Office', this was defined as 'an act of kindness or attention.'

He returned to his own country forthwith, having discovered that the office was not where he was to live, (neither, unlike the USA, was the Home) and there was very little kindness and even less attention there.

The *Oxford English Dictionary* is so important that its definitions, as one salesman repeatedly assured me, are widely accepted in English courts of law. A North American (Mexican) friend, on being informed of this, arrived at London Airport with a copy of the OED and a *cedula* of identity. He told the immigration officer that, as he was not a foreigner, he clearly needed no further documentation or permission to land.

'The detention centre they put me into before deporting me to Mexico City,' he told me, 'not to mention the pie, gravy and mashed potatoes and the astonishing tabloid newspapers kindly supplied, cured any desire to assert my Britishness, whatever the OED might say. I think that that was partly, at least, intended by the authorities.'

The Home Office may not have any control over the OED, or a grasp of the finer nuances of the English language, but they certainly know how to deal with people whom they feel to be foreigners. Citizens of the United States may not have it so rough, may not be commonly regarded as foreigners, but they are undoubtedly also aliens by law in the UK.

Has the OED got it wrong? I ask myself again. Hardly: by its own confession, the *Oxford English Dictionary* (its advertising claims) is 'the ultimate authority on the usage and meaning of English words and phrases'.

Indeed, it is more: it does not conceal from us that it is actually 'the ultimate reference book'. Bearing in mind the fact that the English are famed for their modesty and reticence, the OED must therefore be *even more* than the Ultimate ... although it claims no more than ultimacy. (It defines this word, by the way, as 'lying [sic] beyond all others'. And again, perhaps from modesty, it lists no word equivalent to the concept of 'beyond the beyond'.)

When considering all this, I veered slightly from the main orientation of my studies to look at what 'the Americans' thought about the matter. Webster, (*New World Dictionary of the American Language*) was, of course, my authority of first recourse.

Webster, as you will immediately have noted, has done an OED on us, by assuming that gringospeak alone is 'The American Language'. I wondered what the other Americans think of that. But leaving this interesting question for later, I forsook the OED for its American/non-foreign counterpart.

With their English roots, I felt certain, these particular North Americans would be sure to provide entertainment as well as instruction, as promised by their English counterpart. Their dictionary would confidently affirm two or three things adding up to what foreigners were. Yet these would undoubtedly conflict with one another in non-Anglo-Saxon minds.

Well, to work. The American dictionary said:

Foreigner: a person born in another country; alien.
Alien: (1) a foreigner (2) a foreign-born resident who is not naturalized.
American: (1) a native or inhabitant of America.
(2) a citizen of the US.

So, to the Americans (or, at least, according to Webster):
An American [2. a citizen of the United States] can be a foreigner [a person born in another country]. And an American can be someone born in the US, or someone *not* born in the United States — for example in one of the thirty-odd countries of the Americas.

Once in an American city (albeit a Latin one) I had a strange experience involving English people and foreignness. I was living in Buenos Aires, after spending some years in England, and I had met very few English people in Argentina. Apparently, though unaware of it, I had developed a sort of incipient nostalgia for the English language or the people, or both.

One evening walking near the Casa Rosada, I came across a rollicking band of sailors, just off some ship, staggering across the square arm-in-arm and roaring out the well-known English ditty 'Knees up, Mother Brown!'

Something about the sight, or more likely the sound, triggered an automatic reaction. Rushing up to them, imbued with a strange sensation of pleasurable recognition, of delight, I cried: 'Are you English?'

They certainly were; their enthusiasm matched my own, and they swept me back to my hotel, skipping and prancing, calling for a celebration and in a condition of great euphoria.

We rolled into the foyer of the Plaza Hotel in this state of altered consciousness.

At that time I had not read the OED. Hence I did not know that Americans (including of course Latin ones) were not foreigners. If I had then had the benefit of the OED, the *Argentinos*, authoritatively defined as non-foreign, would, surely, have been English enough for me. I should have regarded the sailors as just another bunch of ill-behaved transients. And I would therefore have been saved the embarrassment soon to be caused by my guests.

In a matter of minutes our merry band was installed in the hotel's copper-lined dining-room, where the seafarers competed in pouring crushed ice from the bowls of fruit down one anothers' necks, calling for alcohol, female company and more.

Requested to leave, they quite naturally shouted, repeatedly and in unison, 'No way, José!'

As they began to carve their initials on the chairs and I saw the twitching face of the head waiter, I somehow began to think of *them* as less than perfect.

My mind did a somersault and I still remember my explanation to the infuriated *Maître*. The words came out as if automatically: '*Son Ingleses, extranjeros, gente sin instrucción, Señor ...*'

English, foreigners, people without education ... 'Barbarians without lineage, *Caballero*', he murmured gravely in agreement, his face now impassive, as he sent a bus-boy for the hall porter to summon the *policia*.

The earliest OED citation of the word 'foreigner' is from 1413. By 1711, Jonathan Swift (in *Thoughts on Various Subjects*) was insisting that foreigners, even extra-terrestrials, were to him only people from another part of the same town:

> 'Whoever live at a different end of the town from me, I look upon as persons out of the world, and only myself and the scene about me to be in it.'

But how typical is this, after all? Was the Irishman Swift just amusing himself, or lampooning the English?

After all, it was this same Dean Swift who wrote:

> 'The English are the most disgusting form of little odious vermin that have ever infested any quarter of the globe.'

But, either way, the *Oxford English Dictionary* gives us the assurance that, certainly in 1875, the word foreigner could actually mean 'a stranger, a person who comes from any other county but Sussex.'

So an American *is* a foreigner after all: the OED shows that it can have it both ways. Yet we still know little more than that a foreigner is probably a person from somewhere else.

Mind you, the OED bills itself as 'instructive as well as entertaining', so perhaps here it is simply being entertaining. But wait a moment: be careful of facile assumptions. *A person*? I did say 'a person' from somewhere else. Now, do we even know that a foreigner *is* a person?

We do not. A foreigner need not be a person at all, as Oxford insists, backing the contention with this nineteenth-century quotation:

> 'The black rat and the common mouse are enumerated . . . but both these are foreigners, imported by the shipping.'

Foreign, whatever else it may stand for, certainly does not carry with it many connotations which any self-respecting Englishman would be likely to admire or respect, if the authoritative English *Thesaurus* of Roget is anything to go by. Searching for what *Roget's* calls a Topic, we find under Foreigner:

> 'alien, stranger, continental, barbarian, Celtic, fringe, lime-juicer, greaser, dago, wog, paleface, gringo, Martian, resident alien, metic, uitlander, expatriate, migrant, emigrant, immigrant, declarant, refugee, deracinée, displaced person, DP'.

So, as with so many other things English (and British) there is almost unlimited scope for being or dealing with foreigners, even for calling almost everyone else a foreigner.

The *Thesaurus* would, it seems, even allow the word 'paleface', generally thought to include Englishmen, to signify Foreigner.

Or 'expatriate', commonly used in the media to mean an English (or British) person working abroad. Given this remarkable brief, let us now hasten to see how the English handle foreigners.

To sum up: an American is and is not a foreigner; an animal is a foreigner if a black rat or common mouse; an Englishman, even, may be a foreigner (if he is, for example, a Paleface).

None of these, however, seems to be a foreigner if he, she or it comes from Sussex: though things may have changed there since 1875.

Since a foreigner can be almost anyone or anything, or nobody or nothing, we can now begin to descry, however dimly, the immense scope and complexity which the English bring to their dealings with foreigners.

Not to mention our sympathy with the English tourist abroad. This is the one, of course, who − hearing himself referred to as a foreigner − cried 'I'm not foreign, I'm English!'

And to think that, for centuries, instead of being seen as subtle and obviously deep-thinking, these English people have been sorely traduced, even imagined to be thick-witted.

The rest of the world has for long believed that when faced with a foreigner, the English reaction has been limited to talking, slowly, in English, in a loud voice. It's more likely that they have been busy adopting Roget's twenty-five names for the foreigner − or inventing their own.

I am happy to announce that an English grammarian has confirmed that my own coinage of *Meticology* will adequately cover the present enterprise, the Study of Foreigners.

'*Metic*' is an English word (or, at least, a word found in English dictionaries and in Roget) to denote a foreigner. Like almost everything else English, as I discovered and noted in *Darkest England,* it is of foreign origin: in this case Greek. Its derivation is, says *Chambers's*, from the Greek for someone who has changed his or her house, a 'resident alien'.

Of course, the British have been *dealing* with foreigners, with greater or lesser success. So it is high time that we had a handbook such as this, embodying the results of meticological endeavour for those in need of them, whether English or otherwise.

Of course, we have to make certain assumptions, which could turn out to be fallacious. For example: is an Englishman a man as we know men? I only ask because, according to *The Daily*

Telegraph, a 'Briton' is evidently not a human being at all. I have kept a cutting from the *Telegraph* and there you find what would seem to the foreigner a quite unequivocal headline:

'MAN ACCUSED OF KILLING BRITON'[2]

There is always something new (to the foreigner) coming out of England. If, like me, you imagine that things cannot be changed, be informed immediately that reality itself, facts themselves, are being changed in England every day.

My evidence? There is tons of it. I limit myself, to spare you fatigue, to another report from *The Daily Telegraph*.

The paper's Travel Correspondent reveals here that British Rail, plagued by late trains, scrapped some timetables.

The result: since there is no fixed time of arrival or departure, no train can be called 'late'.[3]

1

The Questions They Ask

'Advice is seldom welcome; and those who
want it most always like it least.'
                                    — Lord Chesterfield

Foreigners are well known for asking such infuriating questions
as 'Is England in Britain or Britain in England?'

They want to know where Britain is, and who the Brits are;
and what connexion, if any, all this has with the United Kingdom
or Great Britain. And this isn't only among the this-is-Tuesday-
we-must-be-in-London-England brigade. I have even been asked,
in America by what is known there as 'an educator', where in
Britain the UK (pronounced Ukk) is. When I denied all knowledge
of such a place, I was treated as an impostor and disinvited from
a barbecue being held by the State Governor.

An Australian conman, overhearing the Ukk question, and
quicker-witted than I, waded straight in. 'The UK is a part of
London, near Earl's Court, and its inhabitants are called Ukkies',
he told a riveted audience of New England socialites. (Someone
forgot to lock up the gubernatorial silver coffee-spoons, and the
Aussie got away with them, I am glad to report.)

As an English man or woman, you will regularly be annoyed
by foreign questions. You will probably want to answer: 'We are
English, and that is enough. After all, the French are French and
the Italians are Italians; why can't we be the same, at least to
some extent? We are, you know, in Europe now.'

You may, too, be inhibited by the trace-memory of a thing
called the Race Relations Act. For those many English people
who don't know about it, I summarise that it is some kind of
a law which keeps getting dragged up in the newspapers and
prevents some people from speaking their minds, while

encouraging others to speak theirs. Someone once got into trouble with it by advertising for a Scotsman to cook porridge – that kind of thing.

Or it may just be a case of stiff upper lip, and a disinclination to be a general-information bureau. After all, it has taken centuries for the various meanings and nuances of Englishry to develop. I suggest referring people to a dictionary. You can most easily do this by claiming not to be able to understand the question or the foreigner's accent. In any case, any good English dictionary will afford hours of harmless fun.

British, it says in one, refers both to the old inhabitants of these islands and also to the *non-British people* who came after them. Also that 'Briton' means 'A Welshman'. Since 'welsh' also means 'foreigner', you'll see what I mean by fun. And, you may be glad to know, the foreigner will discover from the pages of that same authority that he is himself

> 'Alien: extraneous: not belonging: unconnected: line not appropriate.'

And all without your having to say a word, or express any opinion.

Your foreigner is already walking on eggs. Even 'foreignness' includes 'want of relation to something: remoteness', and is confidently traced to its origin in 'out of doors'. The Englishman's home is his castle, remember. This seems to be the reason why out of doors is so remote and has no relation to 'something'.

Those English people – they are surely very few – who have felt trepidation at a possible encounter with a foreigner may now see how unfounded such feelings really are. The foreigner is not likely to be much of a problem: not in the long run, anyway. And not where his confusion about the Island Race is concerned. You can readily confuse him several times more effectively than he could ever confuse you. English people have centuries of practice at this.

A question asked of Frank Barrett in the Dordogne was reported by him in *The Independent*. A French couple found their British guests hard to follow:

> 'We were all very polite,' said the *patronne*, 'but why did the British never seem to be enjoying themselves on holiday? They always seemed so *distrait*, so intense.'

I have noticed this, too. When giving a lecture, if I see the sea of faces lose all expression, or become slightly twisted, as if struggling with an idea – I know I am going to get a great deal of applause. They *must* have been enjoying themselves. This must have something to do with the supposed habit of taking their pleasures sadly.

Mind you, I think that one of the reasons the English (and other Brits) are concentrating so hard, even when on holiday, is that they are trying to solve some of the problems that also bedevil visitors. These certainly take some solving.

An English person could tell at a glance the difference between jam and marmalade. But he or she would be hard put, as I was when closely questioned the other day, to tell a foreigner what that difference actually is. It is, apparently, not enough to say that the preserve is made with oranges, lemons or limes, since the word marmalade itself comes from 'quince or honey apple'.

Or, again, how do you know when to say 'the middle of the road' or 'the centre of the road'? This was worrying an English friend recently. He works in Russia, and rang me up from there to see whether I could help him answer a Slavic perplexity about the matter.

A German asked me why British Telecom has a telephone number which you can ring if your telephone is NOT working. What, he wanted to know, do you do if you cannot ring because your instrument is out of order?

A Dane writes to ask why it is obligatory to carry canines on the London Underground. Being a good Scandinavian he also wondered why so many people were ignoring the sign:

'DOGS MUST BE CARRIED ON THE ESCALATORS'

2

Aversion Therapy

'If the English did not exist, it would not be
necessary to invent them.'
— Attributed to Charles de Gaulle

Most nationalities boast about themselves. There is a certain
amount of this among the English. However, there is also so much
running themselves down that one has to suspect that the motive
is a kind of aversion therapy. Its aim is to deter all but the bravest
from visiting the country. One can imagine, deep in the secret
English Policy Determination Headquarters bunker, the sign:

'MAKE ANNOUNCEMENTS TO DETER VISITS BY
FOREIGNERS.'

The press, it would appear, are the principle tool. I too have
been in my bunker — making an exhaustive study of a selection
of cuttings stretching back over twenty years. The pattern is
unmistakable. Britain, we are told, is terrifying place. The people
are dreadful and there is little worth seeing anyway. The sensible
foreigner had far better stay at home. Especially when:

PILOTS 'RISKING LIVES' BY DRINKING,

shouts a report in *The Sunday Times*;

Heavy drinking is endangering the health of British airline
pilots and putting passengers at risk, an international study
has revealed ...
British pilots drink more than their counterparts anywhere
in the world, with one in eight consuming the equivalent of
31 whiskies or 15 pints of beer a week. Only one in 28 is
teetotal.

Of course, our foreigner may avoid this hazard by travelling to Britain on a foreign airline — perhaps an Islamic, completely teetotal one. There is, however, another line of defence — the people. Adrian Woodridge, in *The Daily Mail* asks:

MAD IN BRITAIN: ARE WE REALLY A BARMY NATION?

He follows up with some stunning information:

'Are we British bonkers? A new survey, laboriously compiled by MORI (Market and Opinion Research International) . . . suggests that we are positively raving. We have little grasp of what is going on around us; and we spend much of our time repeating comforting clichées and meaningless phrases. To the Red Queen in Alice it was an achievement to believe half-a-dozen impossible things before breakfast. To the modern Briton, it seems, this is not even a challenge . . . Along with self-delusion, self-contradiction seems to be a national vice. One in four Tory supporters said they would like to see a socialist society. The very people who blame crime on lack of parental discipline claim that they are not worried about the rise in illegitimacy. Nine out of ten people describe themselves as active Christians but fewer than one in five bother to go to church. Many believe in heaven but not in life after death.'

Before he can meet people to verify that report, our foreigner may have to brave Heathrow Airport, a place so impossible it has driven even residents to emigrate. 'The Weasel' in *The Independent Magazine* says:

'I once asked Graham Greene why he had decided to leave England, and he replied that he couldn't stand the sound of braying English middle-class voices, particularly at Heathrow Airport . . .'

Mind you, a visitor who *did* find his way to England would be doing well, by English standards. A *Sunday Times* poll[1] found that one in six of the population could not find Britain on a map. So it seems as if several million Britons do not know where they are.

If and when he does penetrate the charmed circle of English

culture, he will find life here odd enough to make him wish to leave at once — or stay forever.

He may travel by the Tube, the London Underground railway transport system. Visitors note, with pleasure, that the name of many a station is lettered in an almost continuous band, all along the upper part of platform walls. It seems designed to allow passengers to read the station's name from any part of the train. An excellent idea: the only problem is that the windows of the trains are set just too low for the lettering to be visible. So, the name cannot in fact be read at all, unless you are standing directly by the doors when they are opened.

In the rush hour (when you need most to know where you are) the name is obliterated even from that position by the throng of passengers entering and leaving the train.

I approached an official to find out what the explanation could be. He was a London Transport employee, who described himself as 'A Jamaican Englishman', and he explained:

> 'They make the trains too low, or perhaps the rails. Or maybe both. On the other hand, perhaps they make the writing too high.'

That's all right, then.

In spite of the Tube's idiosyncrasies, our visiting foreigner may find himself at the Zoological Gardens. Here, according to the Diary of *The Times:*

> 'The iguanas in the London Zoo Reptile House drink from a brown earthenware bowl of the kind available at any pet shop. The bowl even has "DOG" in large black lettering on its side.'

So what impression does all this make on the hapless foreigner? The British Tourist Authority — which asked foreigners at ports of exit for their views — revealed that the departing visitors found the country 'exotic'. A description, says *The Standard* reporting this, more usually applied to Bali or the Seychelles.

(British newspapers seem to me to have an alarming propensity to treat their readers as imbeciles. I wonder how many London commuters, reading their evening paper, did NOT know that Bali or the Seychelles were considered more exotic than Britain? And just after the Gulf War, a major English newspaper published a huge photograph of a portrait of Saddam Hussein riddled with bullet holes. The caption said 'A picture of Saddam Hussein, riddled with bullet holes'. There is, though, something rather endearing, sort of small-town, about this.)

However, to resume: Why do the foreigners call Britain exotic? Because, we are informed, they have to cross the water to get here. But, surely, people cross water to reach all manner of destinations which could hardly be described as exotic. Do the Maltese find France, across the sea, exotic? Or the Turks, journeying to Spain, how do *they* feel?

I decided to conduct my own informal poll at a major British airport. First, I asked a bunch of Danish students at Gatwick if they would call England exotic. They roared with laughter, and one said, 'Many thanks! That's a nice, polite way of putting it. We'll certainly use that one.'

They moved off, towards Passport Control, and my attention was seized by a tiny, rumpled figure. He plucked at my sleeve, and I noticed that he was wearing a clerical dog-collar.

'Why, oh, why do they do it, *Monsieur*?' he almost sobbed.

From this I inferred that he was French. I forgot the old English proverb 'Think today and speak tomorrow' and immediately addressed him:

'Is it the English, *mon brave*?'

'It is, indeed. Why, oh, why . . .'

'Why what?'

'Why do they demote me, just because I am a Catholic?'

'Can they do such a thing?'

'Assuredly. I am a *curé*, which means in English "vicar", but they call me curate, which in French is only *vicaire*. If I call myself "vicar", I am demoting myself to curate . . .'

It is, I agree with the Frenchman, pretty rum when you come to think of it that the British take other people's titles and reverse their meaning. But it clearly is an excellent way of dealing with foreigners.

Knowing that the English are not all keen to have their country flooded with visitors, even ecclesiastical ones, I added my mite to the aversion therapy evidently aimed at the French clergy.

'*M. le Curé*,' I said, 'you are evidently poorly informed as to the conditions which obtain in this peculiar island.'

'I am, indeed,' he said, 'but I am burning to understand.'

'There is an old English proverb,' I continued, 'to the effect that "Zeal with knowledge is a runaway horse".'

'Horse?'

'Yes, indeed,' I went on, having stirred in, as you will have noticed, a measure of confusion; 'horse is the least of it. Have you not heard of the lack of human rights in England? Why, anything might happen to you ...'

If he had been worried before, he really was disturbed now.

'Human rights?'

'Human rights. Have you not read the sage words of Anthony Lester, QC, Chairman of the International Centre for the Protection of Human Rights?'

'No, I have not ...'

'He says that even citizens of Britain "unlike most other citizens of Europe, continue to be denied speedy and effective remedies before their own courts for breaches of their basic rights and freedoms by the state and its agents."'

'Even their own citizens?' he gasped.

'Even their own citizens.'

It took him some time to recover sufficiently to ask the routine question about whether England was in Britain or Britain in England. I ignored it and hit him again with another peculiarity of the English which I hoped would be decisive.

'Do you know about their hedges?' I demanded.

'Their hedges?'

'Yes, hedges, *Les haies!*'

'No', he said, weakly, 'but tell me about them.'

Drawing from my wallet a cutting from the bunch which I keep for emergencies (to combat logical foreigners) I read:

'Fison's HEDGESETTER was the answer to a gardener's prayer — a chemical that slowed the growth of privet hedges so that they needed to be cut only twice a year.'

The Frenchman was clearly impressed. 'The perfidious ones are assuredly clever inventors,' he allowed.

'Yes,' I told him; 'and the account from the London newspaper *The Mail on Sunday* continues:

'But it was quietly dropped in 1972 after the Company found that gardeners LIKED cutting hedges.'

That really did for him. He took the next flight back to Paris.

Today's newspapers are full of accounts of the millions spent every year in policing the foreigners who seek to enter Britain. If the English had the courage of their convictions, they would brief their officials with the contents of this book, and save a fortune every day.

Come to think of it, I am thinking of stationing myself permanently at a London airport, and doing my own stint towards this laudable cause.

3

The French

'He is not laughed at who laughs at himself'
— English Proverb

Many English people insist that dealing with the French can't be done at all.

On the other hand, it *has* to be done; the Channel Tunnel is in operation, the Continent is no longer cut off. As we saw in my dealings with the French vicar, the weapon of first choice should certainly be illogicality. The French pride themselves on their clear and rational thinking. The English, they believe, are confused and confusing. Very well: let battle commence.

Geoffrey Wheatcroft, one of London's brightest journalists launched a typical broadside:

'Our mean and peevish, drizzling and damp little island avoids the '*cher maître*' superstition of France, where every obvious charlatan is revered and every modish fad is greeted with childlike credulity.'[1]

Remember: English people tend to believe that their country has never been conquered or invaded. Most know, of course, that the Danes, Norwegians, Romans, Celts, Saxons and French did occupy the place. But the fact that the Spanish Armada didn't make it somehow seems to blot out the rest. Many members of the community would agree with Judge Michael Argyle who is credited with saying:

'There have been many attempted invasions of the United Kingdom since 1066 and they have failed ...'

It is unclear exactly what United Kingdom is being referred to; the UK we know and love did not exist in 1066. It only came

24

into existence on 1 January 1801 (*Haydn's Dictionary of Dates*), if then. By the way, it is said that the phrase was never officially laid down by any governmental authority or document and so the country under this name may not actually exist yet.

When you research it, you find, bingo! there *has* been an invasion recently in historical terms — and it was a successful one. Britain today could be said to be built on it. But the Dutch-mercenary troops of William of Orange who became an English king simply do not impinge on the public consciousness. English people are always taught that the military operations and occupation of 1688-91 were 'The Glorious Revolution', run by foreigners, after which there was a Bill of Rights, and Parliament reigned supreme.

But, a foreign King, (Scottish-French-Danish-German), a European army, an occupation, to achieve English freedoms? The truth, says Jonathan Israel, is 'dramatically different' from the official British version, believed by virtually all. He tells us:

'In reality England (and later Ireland) was invaded by a large and well-trained foreign army, initially 21,000 men but later increased, that was brought here in November 1688 on 500 ships — an armada four times larger than the Spanish Armada of 1588. This vast strategic exercise drew additional troops and resources from Germany and Scandinavia and was undertaken in collusion with several other Protestant and Catholic powers.'[2]

Nor is that all:

'The invasion was planned and organised long before a tiny group of unrepresentative, and not particularly important English dissidents sent their so-called "invitation" to the Prince of Orange. And although William led the invasion, he had very limited powers in the Dutch Republic ...

'The Dutch army landed in Devon and gained military control of southern England. It had little assistance from the English rebels.'

Our authority continues:

'Readers will not find a word about the next episode in any British school, university, text-book or standard work. But the truth is that when the Prince of Orange marched in triumph into London, in December 1688, he did so after ordering all the remaining English troops in the capital to withdraw a minimum of 20 miles from the city. The bulk of the Dutch army was brought into, or placed around, London; Dutch Blue Guards took up all the posts around Whitehall and Hyde Park; and London remained under Dutch military occupation for 18 months . . . In effect the King of England [James II] was deported by the Prince of Orange and a foreign army, from his own land.'

The British had to repay William for the expenses of this adventure, out of taxation. And he didn't even have the pretext that he was the legitimate successor to the throne, as William of Normandy could claim, on any legal grounds.

The near-naturalisation of the Norman occupation causes interest and consternation among the French, particularly intellectuals, who tend to regard Britain as a former colony. They even call the English *'les rosbifs'*, though it was the French themselves who introduced the dish to England. Pointing this out is a simple and effective ploy for dealing with them.

The Times has further tips for its readers. It warns them not to forget 'the golden rule of French officialdom':

'Anything is possible, but first there must be drama. Any request is always met with a curt shake of the head and the phrase: *'Ce n'est pas possible.'*

So, what is one to do? In England, if someone says that something is impossible, that is that. It IS impossible, ninety-nine times out of a hundred. But in France? Well, the article continues:

'That is, of course, merely the opening shot across the bows of a battle which must include much arm-waving, simulated lack of understanding, imputations about one's parentage, remarks about one's countenance, and a final grudging acceptance that yes, perhaps you do have some sort of right to be here, and yes (much shrugging), eyes raised heavenwards, perhaps you will find the right desk over there . . .'

You have to know your opponent, of course, and this

information may be useful with officials. But what do they think of *you*, the Englishman?

I have mentioned the Eurotunnel link between France and England. A director of Eurotunnel's operations was quoted in *The Sunday Telegraph* on his way of dealing with the English:

> 'The British are probably less flexible than the French. If they put up a wall of resistance to a suggestion, the only way to deal with it is to push back, but not to provoke a clash; you do it with a smile.'

So the English have to be firm with the French, and the French with the English. Of course, this book is about How to Deal With. You may wish to annoy or to please the French. If the former, you can tell them that, in England, 'French leave' means going off without proper permission. If the latter, you might quote the old English proverb, recorded by J. Heywood in 1546: 'Jack would be a gentleman if he could speak French'. Quotations are always useful, for good or ill, depending on your intentions.

It is in some ways a pity that you are not a Yank, for the proverb about Yanks is even more flattering to the French: 'When a good American dies, he goes to Paris'. And yet the poor Americans are constantly lamenting: 'We have a love-hate relationship with the French – we love them, they hate us . . .'

Francis Bacon (*Essays: Of Seeming Wise*) gave us an even pithier saying to think about:

> 'The French are wiser than they seem'

he said; which is perhaps intended as a compliment. And the aphorism concludes:

> 'and the Spaniards seem wiser than they are.'

4

The Spanish

Millions of English people spend their holidays in Spain every year. Many – perhaps most – of them seem to come back with only the fuzziest idea of what the Spanish are like.

This is not, in spite of what the tabloid Press insists, because virtually all British tourists are lager louts and drunk all the time. It is mainly, as I have observed on the spot, that they spend all their time with each other. Apart from the time they spend with waiters, who tell them nothing about Spain and – for personal reasons – less about themselves.

So it is not often that English people have to deal with Spaniards, as such. Francis Bacon's Spaniards may seem wiser than they are simply because nobody from England has much contact with them, even in Spain.

But within Spain one has to be careful once one strays beyond the confines of the English pubs in Torremolinos.

In Mallorca, for instance, or Barcelona, people seem loath to call themselves Spanish at all: they are Catalans. I was sitting outside a Palma café one day, reading (from curiosity) a copy of *Arriba*, the Fascist newspaper, when a pedlar approached. When I ignored him, he struck the paper from my hand, calling me a degenerate Spaniard befouling his Catalan homeland.

Again, in Córdoba, I was so fed up with being elbowed off the pavement that I caught hold of a burly pedestrian who was about to push me into the roadway and demanded to know why he was so aggressive.

'You South Americans are all alike!' he shouted (I learnt my Spanish in Argentina). Then he informed me that 'it is no part of our culture to give way in the street, therefore it cannot be polite or rude, and you should learn our ways, in our country.'

Is that really the Spanish way? I asked, slightly bemused by

28

his anthropological approach (he did turn out to be an anthropologist, by the way).

'Spanish?' he snarled, *'absolutamente no!* I am speaking of us, the Andalusians. We are Arabs, you know – none of your Castilian nonsense here!'

So, the stereotypical Spaniard which we might feel we know – or need for our studies – may not really exist at all. And as for the Basques . . . the tall, dark, impulsive, fun-loving Spaniard may well be hard to find in Iberia. Scandinavians, especially, complain that lithe, flashing-eyed señoritas dancing the fandango on tables are fairly rare in that part of Spain.

Many Catalans and Basques choose to speak their own languages in preference to Spanish; so your night-school linguistic ability may go to waste. Likewise the guitar, the mantilla, and the tango. There is even, dare I say, a growing dislike on the part of some for the bullfight.

Still, if you can't deal with a Spaniard as you conceive a Spaniard to be, you can always redefine him as a foreigner.

At a dinner-party recently, I heard a story, told by a Spanish Duchess, which might form the basis of a useful exercise in dealing with foreigners. I am still puzzled, however, about whether it is designed to illustrate how well the British can manage foreigners: or to show the combination of stiff-upper-lip and insensitivity which is so often (of course wrongly) attributed to them. People who, in the English phrase, 'dine out' on narratives may well find it useful to make them open-ended.

Anyway, the Duchess said:

'A Spaniard was drowning in the sea, having just fallen off a yacht at a harbour's edge, where water is often deep.

'As he came up for the third time, he espied an Englishman whom he knew, just disembarking from his own yacht. Luckily he was within hailing distance. The Spaniard had enough breath left to bellow: "I can't swim!"

'The Englishman stopped, turned towards the Spaniard and shouted, "*Do* be quiet! *I* can't play the violin, but you don't hear *me* yelling all over the place about it . . ."'

5

The Americans

'I am willing to love all mankind, except an American.'
– Dr. Johnson, *The Life of Samuel Johnson*[1]

The Brits call all Anglo-Saxon North Americans 'Yanks'. This is a mistake – the Southerners hate the tag and snarl when they hear it. Canadians are North Americans, too, but they like it even less than the Southerners if you call them Americans.

You can tell the difference between Canadians and United States citizens, however, by a simple test. Get your candidate to say 'How now, brown cow'. The Canadian is the one who says his or her 'ow' rather like the people of Oxfordshire or Bucks do in England.

In any case, I shall feel free to follow the august example of the OED and refer to United States citizens as 'Americans'.

As the English have discovered, the best way to deal with the (United States) Americans is to confuse them with words. Since the UK and USA usages are often different, you can achieve a great deal at negligible cost.

Americans are generally credited with trying to impress you. If you suspect this, await your chance. For some reason, this next ploy works well with name-droppers.

When your American says, for instance, 'I was invited to stay at the Kennedy home . . .' interrupt at once. Your opportunity has arrived. As you know (and the American probably doesn't) when an Englishman refers to a (something) 'home' he almost always means an institution, which is no such thing. Indeed, it's likely to be something like a facility for the psychologically disadvantaged, as in 'you'd be far better off in a home'.

30

All you need to say is, 'What were you diagnosed as having, then?' in a very sympathetic tone.

You can carry on with reminiscences about sad cases you have known, until he has roared out his disclaimer. Then all you need to say is: 'Home? You mean . . . Oh, I see: I'm awfully sorry.'

By then, of course, it is too late for your name-dropper to retrieve the situation.

Mud sticks. However unjustly, there will be some people present at any social occasion where this gambit is played who will be vaguely sure forever after that at some time your unfortunate American was not exactly a hundred cents on the dollar.

The dollar. Americans concur with the English in accepting this unit of exchange as of paramount importance. English people will often refer to '64,000-dollar' questions, just as if this old Teutonic unit were still their own . . . Dealing with Americans, especially on their home turf, requires a proper familiarity with it.

In the first place, it is pronounced *daala*. A *daala* is divided into 100 cents. These are often called pennies although, of course, they are not pennies at all.

One *daala* is also divided into 20 *nikulz*, which are equal to ten *dymz* – because a *nikul* is 5 pennies and a *dym* is ten pennies.

For some reason yet to be determined, the *daala* is derived from the German Thaler (as is the penny from the pfennig) but the cent is taken from the French: research into this anomaly continues.

Since you, the English, have got rid of the guinea, crown, half-crown, florin, groat, and so on, you can afford to be fairly complacent about money when dealing with Americans . . .

Now, of course I know that much British 'small' change is so heavy that mending trouser pockets has become a growth industry. And that other coins, such as the five-pence piece, are so small that the newspapers warn against letting small children choke on them. But you are in with a chance when scoring points about currency. If in doubt, as the English saying has it, bluff it out . . . Attack is the best form of defence.

Money is serious in America. We almost automatically started to deal with money as soon as the subject of America came up, in conformity with the rule, often heard in Britain:

No conversation about the United States ever lasts for more than three minutes without the word 'dollar' being involved.

It is equivalent to the pious exclamations which pepper conversations in other cultures. Because of the seriousness of the whole subject, you can alarm most Americans or at least catch them off-balance by speaking of their currency as 'quaint'. Then go on a bit about *daalas* and *quarras* and so on. Quaintness has its cherished place in all our hearts.

The quaintness of the American Ambassador, some years ago, has not yet passed off. People still tell the tale, at dinner parties, of his referring in front of Queen Elizabeth to the 'elements of refurbishment' at his London home. The only people of England likely to understand this kind of English are ordinarily steered away from her Majesty.

On the subject of homes, there is an English anecdote which is attributed to many Americans, including Joseph Kennedy. Legend has it that it happened while he was United States ambassador to the Court of St. James's. The story goes that the Ambassador had just finished looking over a stately home he was thinking of renting for a country retreat in one of the shires.

'Yes, the place seems okay to me', he is reported as saying. Then he saw, over the imposing doorway, the words carved in stone in gothic script: EAST, WEST – HOME'S BEST!

Continued the Ambassador: 'Of course, that guy Home's gotta take his advertisement down ...'

Americans complain, with some justification, I think, that when they are direct they are charged with being uncouth, and when they try to fit in, they are called poseurs. Perhaps they should stick to being professional at whatever is their speciality.

Or maybe not. 'The word "professional"' says a serious journal in my library, 'always betokens, in England, something slightly distasteful ...'

Then again, in today's *Evening Standard*, a leading article speaks of the 'quiet, steady professionalism [of the British] which might, perhaps, be emulated by the brasher Americans.'

Perhaps the problem arises because the two peoples use the same words in different ways. I have seen Americans in polite society in London appalled by a phrase which is quite innocuous to the English: 'Keep your pecker up, old thing!'

The usages are so intricate that they might almost constitute a different language. Certainly in 1978, a noble Lord during a debate is on record as saying:

'If there is a more hideous language on the face of the earth than the American form of English, I should like to know what it is.'

Americans may take comfort from the fact that even English in England is getting a little out of hand. For instance, I have just heard British TV's Channel Four News repeat seven times in an hour the phrase: 'former Indian Prime Minister'. There were several foreigners present. All of them wondered what nationality the 'former Indian' now was. And a mass-circulation tabloid constantly writes of British 'ex-patriots', bemusing foreigners as well as the expatriates themselves.

Baroness Thatcher, known to be keen on good grammar, must wince when she reads that one. But it perhaps does not give her such unease as the not uncommon phrase 'Margaret Thatcher, former British Prime Minister'.

One broadsheet I have just been shown has an educational section for younger readers. There is an article on GREAT CIVILISATIONS, pointed out to me by a seven-year-old. In 'All About the Sioux', I learn: 'More often than not, the settlers attacked the Sioux first, believing they were defending themselves.' Believing that the Sioux were defending themselves, I am being asked; or that the settlers were?

If no occasion for linguistic campaigning arises, you can always score over the Americans by steering the conversation towards the CIA. The intelligence outfits in the USA spend about 30 billion dollars a year. Refer casually to the brilliant plot to poison Fidel Castro's beard, or to the Bay of Pigs invasion, and perhaps to the lack of a warning that Saddam was about to invade Kuwait.

If all this is going a little too far (if you see a CIA-glint, say, in your vis-à-vis's eye) you can always use a traditional English damage-limitation formula.

Say: 'Oh, I was talking about the "other CIA".'

This is what the Culinary Institute of America, of Hyde Park, New York, is called. Completely different, of course, from the crew over at Langley, Virginia.

You can confuse matters sufficiently by alluding to the fact that the cooking school has a fresco of the Last Supper. This is boarded up for safekeeping, as revealed by *Time Magazine* ('Spooks? No, Good Cooks').

Americans (USA variety) have been complaining for years that the test for a Third World country is whether people are anti-American. The Brits haven't quite got that far yet; but there are signs that they're learning.

During the Gulf War Britain was perhaps the closest ally of the United States. But you couldn't have told that by some of the parliamentary debates.

> The major airlines began skirmishing Wednesday to capture frightened American passengers for their half-empty planes ... Robert Adley, a Conservative MP, huffed, 'The Americans think they own the Atlantic and regard transatlantic travel as their fiefdom. The main cause of the slump is the pathetic behaviour of Americans who believe that Baghdad is 43 miles from Piccadilly Circus.'[2]

The Times produced a leading article, AMERICANS AFRAID. Recalling that the term 'great American wimp' was current during Reagan's presidency, the article called American ideas about personal danger 'ludicrous'. Most Americans, it roared, 'are much safer abroad than at home'.[3]

But, it must be noted that none of the foregoing may work. This is because American culture has enough Anglo-Saxon content to enable Americans to run themselves down rather as the Brits do. So they may laugh appreciatively at your attempts to put them down.

6

The Lights — and the Dogs!

Tea and curry. The British brought tea to India
from China, and Europeans brought curry, as
a medicine, from Central America: chillies were
unknown to us, and first mentioned here in the
sixteenth century. 'Indian' music, according to
our own historians, is Western: it came from
Greece. *Yunani* (Ionian) medicine is not native
to us. The next thing will be the British selling
us back our own antiquities.

         — B. K. Sen[1]

I was standing with my back to the warmth of the baked-potato
stall in Bermondsey Market, south of the Thames. It was pitch-
dark: not surprising in midwinter at five o'clock in the morning.

All around was bustle in the huge open-air car park not far from
Tower Bridge where the Caledonian Market is now held, as the
stallholders unpacked, gossiped, gulped tea from vacuum flasks,
and looked at each other's stock with the help of flashlights.

I moved closer to a knot of men, surrounding a fat woman
who was revealing, slowly and tantalisingly, one piece of jewellery
after another, peeling off its many times used, crinkled newspaper
wrapping.

'Excuse me,' I said, 'what are you gentlemen doing?' At this
distance, the question and its phrasing sound maladroit. But, at
that time, on that freezing winter's morning, it was about as much
as I could manage.

I was trying to break into a layer of British society which, only
a short time before, had been unknown to me. It felt very strange
indeed, very foreign in comparison to, say, Bond Street: not so
far out if likened to the great open-air bazaar in Bombay, or even

35

the one outside Budapest. Far better than the markets of Paris, Nice or Amsterdam: which must explain why there are often so many Continentals there on Fridays. That and the fact that it is featured in most guide-books and tours; German and Italian junkets are often organised to visit London for no other reason than to scour the markets.

There was a light drizzle, and even my Afghan golden karakul fur cap was hard put to keep up with the local version of the British Temperate Climate, as characterised in all UK geography schoolbooks. You may be sure that Bermondsey, together with Covent Garden, are always the coldest places in London.

Nobody took any notice of me at first, so I repeated my enquiry: 'What are you gentlemen doing?'

A huge, really tall fellow, in a shabby warm British Army surplus overcoat and with a beaten-up face like a boxer's (many people in London markets seem either very small or very tall) provided the reaction, if not the answer. He suddenly swung around and grabbed the collar of my Rohan padded jacket.

'Wouldn't you just like to know?' he snarled. It was one of those moments which seem to pursue me almost wherever I happen to be, when I feel myself on the brink: not of the discovery I hoped for, but of some sort of imminent physical rearranging.

Another man, clutching a handful of gaudy, imitation-pearl necklaces, flashed a light on me. I felt the surge of his garlic breath, blended with whisky, against my cheeks. He grinned in the half-shadow.

'Aw, lay off him,' he said, 'it's only Eddie the Persian.'

That was good enough. The burly man relaxed and let me go: 'Hello, Eddie.' He turned back to the jewellery.

I was thankful that I had spent some previous daylight hours the week before in reconnaissance, following a friend's advice to get to know the geography and introduce myself to as many people as possible by a *nom de guerre*.

I had spoken Persian to a Kurd in this market last time, and the Kurd's neighbouring stallholders had instantly manufactured my nickname. After that I had sprinkled it around as I asked prices and admired the piles of silverware, ceramics, *bric-à-brac* – and sheer grot.

In London markets, once people know your name – or the name you are using – they are at ease with you: up to a point.

It's rather like the belief in some cultures (the 'Rumpelstiltskin theme') that knowing a person's name gives you some sort of hold or claim over them.

I had created an unnecessary mystery and, I felt, a certain amount of near-suspicion in Portobello Road by telling some people that I was called Ebenezer MacGillicuddy. Like a visitor to a far-away place, I had perpetrated an unintended discourtesy, broken a taboo, flouted convention.

Some later said that they thought I was a grass, a police informer, others that I was from the tax office, and others that I must be up to something else, equally unacceptable or odd. The more charitable — or perhaps the more imaginative — even suggested that I was an eccentric millionaire or political refugee.

In most other UK company it is almost rude to ask anyone's name directly. Even if you say, trying to be elliptical in the English manner, 'How do you spell your name? I've forgotten,' they are liable to answer 'The usual way'. It's almost as bad as asking people what they do. Young girls at posh schools are still told the cautionary tale of the lady at the cocktail party. She was asked: 'What does your sister do, these days?' The answer, from Princess Margaret, was, of course, 'Still Queen, actually ...'

In the world of London markets it is not quite the same. It is almost as if you are with a different, slightly non-British, tribe. There is a sort of non-English, yet English, jargon spoken by some, as well. If someone makes a call, you are likely to hear this reported as 'I rang him up on the telephone' — as if one could ring up on anything else. Similarly, you may hear, 'I thought in my mind' and 'she is hungry in her stomach'.

If you are putting your goods out for sale in the market, you are 'stalling out'. 'Goodbye' is 'see you later' (however late it is); and the correct response to 'Be lucky!' is not 'Whatever do you mean?' but 'Thanks'.

Although British, the market people behave in a very different way from most others you meet. They are generally cheerful, even when things go wrong — though a few are grumblers and there are some monumental liars. They take up collections for people who are in trouble. They bring each other cups of tea and offer kind words and patience almost beyond belief.

There is a kind of social service in operation. Go to Camden Passage on a Wednesday or Saturday, or to Portobello Road on

a Saturday, and just listen. There you will find people grumbling
or telling the same old story, year in and year out while others
listen politely and with every evidence of sympathy for the
whingers.

Everyone has done 'not too badly' by the afternoon: some have
actually 'taken £7000 before breakfast'; and a few still feel that
you must be from the Mafia or the fuzz.

In winter, few wear warm clothes: and I have not been able
to discover why.

A surprising number of them started in their trade by being
collectors themselves, or merely market-buffs. Bitten by the bug
through 'just looking' they found themselves hooked. Perhaps
the most amazing thing is that so many dealers know very little
about the objects that they are selling. When one draws them
out on some object, knowing full well what it is, they will invent
the most elaborate origins, dates, provenances, without even
superficial plausibility.

I have stood watching this process going on, and I am sure
that it is part of the cultural behaviour of the tribe. The people
asking the details don't expect to get accurate ones, and don't
believe what they are being told. It's not facts, it's conversation.

When I first went to the markets, spotting some Eastern
antiquity whose origins and use I knew well, I used to offer a
full and detailed description to the stallholder. After a bit, I began
to notice that they were not listening, though standing in a polite
posture, and saying 'Ah' and 'Oh' at intervals, while they
surveyed the crowd, combed their hair, or otherwise employed
profitably the time I was wasting.

Then someone explained. 'Things are there to be bought. If
you know what a thing is, you can buy it, or not. What's with
the details?'

Some of the market people spend their winters in Thailand or
the Bahamas; others roar with laughter at the very thought that
they could afford to get away even for a week.

But on that day, some years ago, when I was pretty new to
the market, when I had just become Eddie the Persian, I was
in for a surprise never subsequently to be surpassed in my
marketeering among the Brits. I had taken refuge in a café of
the greasy spoon type, withered with cold, sitting with a hot
chocolate at a table next to a small crouched group earnestly

in converse. As I strained my ears, I distinctly heard the words:

'I'll do what I can, mate, honestly, to get you in. But you haven't seen the lights. And the *DOGS!*'

I was sure that I knew that voice. Slightly squeaky. It had that grammar-school accent trying to copy public-school plumminess. As usual, it sounded, not like plums in the mouth, but like rather small cherries overlaying the south-London intonation.

But the small and stocky figure was a puzzle. He was dressed in quasi-Indian clothes, *shalwar* and *gamis* (which the subcontinentals have looted from Iran and Central Asia). His head disappeared into a Russian-type fur cap and below it was a luxuriant dark, greying beard. I couldn't quite place the man.

Lights and dogs. So, London markets were thieves' hangouts, after all. My head was full of sensational newspaper accounts, constantly rehashed by the Sundays, of how burglars were making fortunes from raiding English country houses and sending priceless garden statues to Italy, pictures to America.

Suddenly (people often seem to act suddenly in market circles: the rest of the time many appear to stand or sit almost motionless) the men got up and left the café. Only the exotically dressed little man remained. He moved over and sat down beside me.

'Yes, I'll have a cup of tea and a couple of smoked salmon sandwiches, darling,' he told the waitress, 'and this gentleman will pay. He's a very old friend: a rich and famous Mexican writer. He won the Nobel Prize, not that you'd know what that was. Got the VC in the War, and swam the Channel three times each way. Quite a lad.'

I did a double-take. I'd only ever met one person who talked like that. Yes, it was . . . none other than my old friend George Archibald Fudge, whom you may have met in my *The Natives are Restless*[2]. The con-man and abbreviationist extraordinary.

'Fudge!' I cried, with delight; 'where have you been, my old mucker?'

'Not so loud, if you don't mind,' he answered, 'and not so much of the Fudge.'

'Why not? And why the amazing clothes?'

'Because I am now Raja Ankabut Fawji: Indo-Pakistani nobleman, antiquities re-exporter and jewel trader. Get a lot of stuff from sales at English country houses. People from British

Raj days dying off, sell up. Indians prize such relics nowadays. Even have their own collectors. Plenty of undeclared rupees sloshing about over there. More future in goods than in notes under the mattress, eh?'

Yes, of course. I remembered how he had used abbreviations to convey meanings they were not intended to have when I was last in contact with him. How he had been CO (not Commanding Officer, but Conscientious Objector) and so on, when I was researching *The Natives*. After all, why not be Fawji?'

'Fawji,' I said, 'you really must do your homework. "Raja" is Indian, "Ankabut" is Arabic, and "Fawji" is Persian.'

'I *have* researched it. All these words are permissible in the subcontinent.'

'But not arranged like that.'

'Yes. In Bombay, where the Muslims, Parsees and Hindus know next to nothing about their own faiths, where Arab traders have been going for centuries and where Persian usages are common, many people speak only English. They do, however, deck themselves out, at times, with extravagant and suchlike names.'

'If you are from Bombay, why "Indo-Pakistani"?'

'Family fled to Pakistan during the Partition, after the War. They were cloth merchants, so I grew up all over the world.'

'Why bring in Pakistan?'

'Because, dear lad, everyone in India or Pakistan can be identified and probably located, both as to origin, family and status, by reference to their home village, town or locality.'

'So?'

'So, everyone has masses of relatives. Except some people who fled to India or Pakistan from one of the other countries during the Partition of the nineteen-forties. A person could be the single survivor of an enormous family.'

I should have known better than to ask. He *had* done his homework.

I asked him about the dogs and the lights. 'If it isn't a rude answer, Fawji, I mean Raja, what was all that about?'

'Don't jump to conclusions, old boy. You may have thought that I was talking about difficult security arrangements: theft, even. Perish the thought! In fact, I am helping those poor fellows to get work on a film set, where there is a movie in the making featuring tiresome dogs. The carbon-arc lights, too, are somewhat onerous.'

'All right, Raja, I believe you — thousands wouldn't. Mind you, people don't dress quite like that anywhere, even in Bombay.'

I needn't have bothered: of course he always had an answer for everything:

'There's an old English saying, "Crooked logs make straight fires", isn't there?'

I asked Fawji to be my guide to the market.

'Tremendously delighted, old son. But what's your name hereabouts?'

'Eddie the Persian'.

'That's just great. But remember, there's quite a lot of Persians around. Can you speak the lingo?'

'Like a native.'

'Good. But where are you supposedly from, over there?'

'City of Mashhad. Identical dialect to the Afghan, few of its denizens actually penetrate here. They tend to be rather religious.'

'Fair enough. Pity you never took up the con game. Might have made something out of you.'

Something of me? Such as ending up at six am on a wet Friday in December, at the age of nearly seventy, dressed as an Indo-Pakistani? I was cold enough to think this nasty thought but, I am happy to report, not quite cold enough to speak it.

Fawji piloted me into the thick of the market.

Three women with American accents were crowding the gangway between two rows of stalls. They were speaking to the man in charge of a stall loaded with what looked to me like junk. He was a tall, sombre-looking fellow with a public school accent and a dirty raincoat.

'Those Victorian vinegar bottles are just *dorlin*!' screamed one woman. Her duvet coat and blue-rinse proclaimed 'Transatlantic' as loudly as her words. The conversation continued something like this:

'Yeah, but he hasn't gotten any in lately, have you, Honey?' said another.

'Back in Texas in our littl' ole' store we could make a killin', if only we could gerrem,' said the third.

They bustled away, and I heard their raucous voices, like

buzz-saws, in full operation a little farther off.

Raja had paused, and was slapping his thigh, though I couldn't see why.

'Pity about the bottles,' I said to the tall man. 'I suppose you could have cleaned up there.'

Now *he* slapped his thigh.

'Where d'ye find this one, Raja?' he asked my friend.

Raja wiped his eyes, and turned to me to explain.

'The point is, that was a little, very small-scale, con-game. They're doing what is called "seeding" in the trade. I don't mind betting that some accomplice of theirs has bought a stock of old vinegar bottles and can't get rid of them. So he's trying to plant the idea, from one stall to another, that a band of crazy American collectors is seeking them. Then he comes round, selling the bottles.'

'But,' I said, 'isn't that a bit naïve? I don't think that I'd be taken in by a trick like that.'

'But you nearly were, friend,' said Raja; 'and it will be played out a bit better than that. For instance, some of the less experienced – or greedier – traders will take the bait and sidle about, asking for vinegar bottles, and will come upon someone who, amazingly, has a stack to sell.'

We moved on. Soon I was looking at three huge, dreadfully badly painted Indian pictures, offered at £150. 'Make me an offer,' wheezed the ageing asthmatic in the World War II flying suit, breaking off his attempts to date an alarmingly made-up, tiny plump blonde of uncertain age standing nearby.

'These are the throw-outs of the ones which you get in Bombay for less than £5 each,' I couldn't stop myself saying.

'Just pay yer fare to Bombay: see wot they'll cost yer then!' shrilled the blonde.

'Nar,' said Flying Suit; 'he's quite royt. I bought 'em there myself, coupla weeks back. They *woz* the throw-outs.'

'Why do you price them so high?' I asked.

'Listen, chum. First, I 'ave ter recoup my investment. Second, these pictures are not for the likes of you. They're for tourists. So shove over, an' give the real punters a chance. Their buses arrive about seven.'

As we walked on, Raja put his hand on my sleeve. 'Listen. You got off lightly that time, because he probably thought that you were a dealer, or because he wanted to impress the blonde. But he might suddenly have turned nasty.'

'And attacked me?'

'Worse than that. Refused to do business with you in future. Believe me, you often find bargains here: that's why there are so many dealers about. Now and again you see something underpriced — could be catastrophically — on someone's stall. Not everyone can know the value of everything: that's where expertise comes in. If you've broken with him, he'll refuse to sell it to you. At the very least, he (or she) won't give you a trade discount. You'd never survive, behaving like that.'

'Is that why everyone always seems to be in such a good humour?'

'Everyone gets on with everyone else; otherwise they don't last here. Call that humour if you like.'

I asked Raja where all this stuff — there seemed to be acres of it — came from.

'Lots from house clearances. Executors usually strip out the valuable stuff. What is left, items of small furniture, cutlery, wall-hangings, ornaments, *bric-à-brac*, less valuable silver and so on, is brought in to the market by house clearers. They get paid for taking the stuff away, too.'

I had recently been attending sales at big London auction houses, Sotheby's, Christie's and the like. I told Raja: 'One thing confuses me. Lots of these faces, standing in front of what look like totters'barrows, in the freezing cold, dressed in nothing special ...'

'Well?'

'Well, I have seen these people, or lots of them, in three-piece suits, buying at swish auctions.'

Raja clasped me on the shoulder. 'You've got it! You see, these boys — and girls — are often more knowledgeable than many up-market dealers. They know more than the Burlington Arcade and Bond Street mob. So they can spot bargains that the bigger guys don't recognise without consulting reference books or specialists. Again, these markets are full of tourists from about 7 or 8 in the morning until 4 or 5 in the afternoon.'

'What about the tourists?'

'Well, when you are travelling in a foreign country, do you go to a market to get an authentic old curio, or do you go to a posh auction? It all boils down to greed and atmosphere. You can often buy cheaper at auctions, but they haven't the atmosphere. It's a matter of selling not only the steak but the sizzle of the steak.'

We stopped at a fast-food stall: most people at markets seem to spend a fair amount of their time eating. As we sipped the tasteless tea, I asked Raja why people so often seemed to know so little about what they were selling.

A very snooty-looking individual with a hooked nose and tattered hat overheard and gave me the answer in a broad Irish accent:

> 'Sure and I'm never paid enough for what I know already; why should I know any more? I'd love to earn commensurately with my education.'

I said to Raja: 'How did *you* get on without any education at all?'

He answered, quick as a flash: 'I had to use my brains instead.'

At this point someone nudged Raja and offered him a bundle of animal horns, Sanskrit manuscripts and viceregal pictures. He hurried off to do business.

After a couple of hours, as I dallied at one stall after another, I began to notice another inexplicable thing. Total strangers would come up to me. Sometimes they would take my hand and shake it cordially.

One said 'It's old bronzes, isn't it? Well, I've something that may interest you ...'

Another called out, as I passed: 'How's the new boat? Made any long-range trips yet? Must cost a bomb to run. Come over here and have a look ...'

A third: 'That lot you got at Bonham's ... Bet you made a packet on it. Must admire your taste and cheek. Here, I've got a couple of paintings I'd like your advice on ...'

I was becoming desperate, since there was no way I could explain, without help, my sudden popularity and supposed recognition.

Finally I tracked down Raja, eating a hot dog on the Triangle, the space adjacent to the main market, which is run by private enterprise rather than by the local Council. I said, 'Raja, perfect strangers are coming up to me and shaking hands. What is going on?'

'Perfectly simple, dear boy. I have passed the word around that you are kosher.'

'That might explain the readiness to trade with me. It does not elucidate why everyone should imagine that I have a special interest in this or that . . .'

Raja nodded sagely. 'Don't you see?'

'No, I don't.'

'Well, here it is. They don't know, and don't care, what your speciality is. They think that by flattering you — calling you an expert on this or that — they will engender a warm glow, which will translate into your looking at what they are really selling. Few really specialise, so if you feel a sense of goodwill towards them as you look at their stuff, you may well buy something.'

'Does it work? Sounds a bit far-fetched to me.'

'Listen. These are some of the best operators in London. Are they going to do something if it doesn't work?'

Flattery will obviously get some people somewhere, in England, as elsewhere.

I wondered where all the treasures I saw piled high on the grubby stalls wound up. I was told that many items from boot-sales, from small antiques shops, from giant open-air events like those at Newark in Nottinghamshire or Ardingly in Sussex and from auctions end up in huge containers bound for the United States or Japan. Germany is another major destination. The dealers say it's because many of its antiques were destroyed in World War II.

Of course, some objects will later be found in Bond Street or Knightsbridge as you might expect. But I discovered another incongruity: I'd always imagined that the quaint curio shops in England's countryside were packed with bargains from country houses. Packed they may be, but very many of them are stocked from London, and they are priced accordingly.

Nor is it entirely true that the British are selling the family silver, as it were, following the eclipse of Empire in the nineteen-fifties. The two major auction houses — Christie's and Sotheby's — were founded in the eighteenth century, before much of the British Empire existed. Rosemary Hill of *The Sunday Telegraph* found out some interesting things:

'A German commentator grumbled that Napoleon's troops were followed everywhere by a correspondingly warlike band of English antique[s] dealers.'[3]

Almost everywhere among 'the trade' there are tales of the newly-rich — Americans looking for family portraits, to pass off as pictures of ancestors when they go back home. There is said to be a good trade in silver which may be described as 'brought over on the *Mayflower*'. It needs to have the right hallmark dating.

This transatlantic tendency is said to date from the nineteenth century. And according to Ms. Hill's article:

'Walpole hung his armour on a dark stairway so that visitors would not notice its disparate origins, and hinted that an ancestor had brought it back from the Crusades.'

Now, Walpole was no nineteenth-century arriviste American. True, he started as plain Mr. Robert, but he became Sir Robert and later Earl of Oxford — and in the eighteenth century he rose to no less a position than British Prime Minister.

So perhaps the British had more part to play than they like to admit in teaching the American tourists in Bermondsey market how to fabricate their origins.

7

Masterly Inactivity

'Is seeing the worst in everything a national
characteristic?'
— Gyles Brandreth,
former MP for the city of Chester

The above question might give the impression that the Englishman
is not sure of himself. My experience of the creature, fortified
by British people I have been canvassing, is that the whole
question of sure and unsure, or of feeling insecure — a largely
recent, American importation — is irrelevant to most of the
English.

A growing number of British people are convinced that self-
questioning is not even American: it has become naturalised there
through the Austrian subculture of Dr. Freud. Although it may
take root in certain sections of the British population (like the
chattering classes or the inhabitants of Hampstead) on the whole
this havering is not something that comes easily. In Britain, (as
in most of the pre-Freud or Vienna-innocent world) it is most
likely to be regarded as a morbid condition. As such, it would
naturally be left to experts for solution, and would certainly form
no part of polite conversation.

Therefore, questions like the one at the top of this chapter are
much more likely to be put strictly for rhetorical reasons — as
yet another weapon in the vast and sophisticated armoury of
techniques for dealing with foreigners.

I don't know, of course, how far the specialised skill of dealing
with foreigners goes back in history. It was certainly in perfect
operation as early as 1066. In that year the people of Kent assessed
the situation, and went out to welcome William the Conqueror
'with green boughs'. Not for them the unnecessary (and widely

47

trumpeted) heroism of the resistance attempted by the English king, Harold.

In consequence, the county of Kent acquired, and still proudly uses, the motto *Invicta*, Unconquered. Technically, of course, this is true: the people of Kent were not beaten in battle, since there wasn't one. If that is not pure genius, I would like to know what is.

This flexibility allows the British to move the goalposts before the hapless foreigner's very eyes. For instance, when challenged by pressure-groups about a refusal to admit refugees, a British high official delivered a most amazing explanation. He insisted they were not exactly refused: they could always get tourist visas and outstay them.

Of course, dealing with foreigners – like handling people inside the country – should have a good dash of delay about it.

There is nothing like delay – stretching things out until everyone has lost interest – to ensure the British point of view prevails. This technique, which they invented, they call Masterly Inactivity.

I vividly recall my daughter Saira, born and brought up in England, returning to culture-shock in Britain. She had been with the *Mujahidin* warriors inside Afghanistan under Soviet rule, and in the Afghan refugee camps.

'The thing about there,' she said, despairing at some seemingly intractable delay, 'is that there you can't get much done without a tip or bribe. But it gets done. Here they won't take bribes, but they won't do it, either!'

The British long ago discovered that foreigners are highly impatient creatures. It is a theme which runs through English literature and humour. Full use is made of this knowledge. I have seen this technique – encapsulated in the great English saying, 'if in doubt, sweat it out' – so often in action, that I can without hesitation rephrase a British motto: 'He who delays, wins'.

The experts are given the tricky matters to deal with (Royal Commissions, Committees of Enquiry, Courts of Law and the rest). They are, however, only distillations from the mass of the people. Everybody in Britain knows how to do it.

You only have to have a blocked gutter, a washing-machine not working, a device not operating, to hear the refrain, echoing through your head, even before you have called the maintenance man:

'You won't get that fixed in a hurry, mate. Dear me, just look at the condition of that! Wot you been doin' to it, eh? You won't get away with under £100, plus tax . . . We're talking about nearer £200 here . . . Of course, I can't come next week, it's a Bank Holiday. Then there's Easter. Of course, the summer'll hold us back a bit. Then, with the holidays, and Christmas coming after that – let's say a couple of years, eh squire?'

This is not only a matter of every British person's experience: the potential for such behaviour lies within him or her too – deeply in, you might almost say built-in. If you want to get something done in England, the following, more complete, calendar is worth consulting, to ascertain when it might actually be finished (or attempted):

JANUARY: Too cold, staff not all back from Christmas and New Year holidays, illness, computer down, we called by but you were not in.

FEBRUARY: Cold and/or fog. Illness, rail tracks frozen, winter holidays, computer down, sudden rush of work.

MARCH: Better wait until after Easter, illness, staff on leave, spare parts not available.

APRIL: Uncertainties due to tax year beginning and ending, computer down, illness, staff shortages.

MAY: Two Bank Holidays cause confusion, computer down, we called but parts not arrived yet.

JUNE: Staff shortages/illness, man broken his leg, transport up the spout, new management, computer down, suggest you wait until it all gets sorted out.

JULY: Holiday season, temporary, skeleton staff only.

AUGUST: As July.

SEPTEMBER: As August and staff not all back yet, computer down, etc.

OCTOBER: Many bad cases of 'flu', weather conditions, spare parts, computer down.

NOVEMBER: Winter holidays coming, staff shortages, soon be Christmas.

DECEMBER: Christmas, broken legs skiing, shortages, transport and computer problems, try in the New Year.

Come to think of it, there may be a brief period, about ten

days or so before Christmas, when it is possible to get a workman
– cash in hand, of course – for your house. This coincides
exactly with the amount of work he needs to buy expensive
computer games for his children's Christmas presents.

Every English person will know all this already. What I am
supplying is the recommendation that the delaying techniques,
so hard-won at home, be used on foreigners. Many foreigners,
on the other hand, will not believe a word of it. So, let me give
an instance for the purposes of documentation.

In 1990 (according to *The Times*) it was calculated that it would
take 400 years for the Council of the London Borough of
Southwark to recover its rent debts. People simply weren't paying.
At that rate, the debt would encompass twelve generations: the
equivalent of the period from the sixteenth century to the present
day.

'Fools rush in' is an English proverb, of course. And yet the
English, characteristically, laugh at the Arab saying, 'Haste is
from the Devil'.

This reflection puts another complexion on a separate matter
quite close to my heart. This is the question of 'There is no such
thing'.

Other foreigners may have noticed that, if you go into an
English shop and ask for something, if it is well-known and out
of stock, you will be told that 'there is no call for it'.

There is a deeper ploy than that, though. If the thing is not
so well-known, you are likely to hear, 'No, there's no such thing'.

This is really clever stuff because it serves two distinct and
powerful purposes: enabling the English person to capture all
the high ground worth having. First, if the shop assistant is able
to state that something does not exist at all, this means almost
absolute power: power to abolish, to permit or deny the very being
of something. Second, it enables said assistant to show that you
are a complete idiot. Who else, after all, would enter a shop and
ask for something which did not exist?

There is one way to counter this. That is, to carry a sample
(an empty bottle, say, or even a photograph) of the item. This,
it is true, will gain a grudging admission that the thing exists.
But, of course, it will not pre-empt the assertion that 'there is
no call for it'. The concurrent shaking of the head, pursed lips
and narrowed eyes combine to establish beyond doubt that

you are probably insane or worse – if there *is* anything worse.

Although I would not say that it is exactly fun to be in the middle of this inspired-delay mechanism, it does mean that your research material is rich and everywhere. After writing the first page of this chapter, I had to go to an electrical appliance shop for a bulb to fit my desk-lamp.

I entered the shop to find the manager standing at the counter, talking on the telephone. He was told to hold, so he asked me what I wanted. I showed him the blown bulb to establish that such things existed. (Once, while attempting to change money from Taiwan I was told by a very large bank near Piccadilly Circus that the 'place no longer existed'.)

The electrician called a grimy youth from the back of the shop. Together they looked at the lamp, as if it were something just landed from outer space. Together they exchanged glances and whistled through their teeth.

'What you think, Fred?'

'I'd get a new one; renew the whole fitting. Old-fashioned, you see. They don't make them any more.'

I said, 'But this *is* new – I bought it here less than a week ago, and you told me it was the very latest thing.'

'Well', said the manager, 'if we *can* replace it, it'll take two weeks at least, then there's ...'

'Easter,' I said.

'Right.'

'Very well,' I said, 'two weeks.' I knew that that would mean a month.

As I left the shop, I heard the manager hollering into the telephone: 'A week to fit a lousy exhaust to my car? It's a blinking liberty, that's what it is ...'

The pace of life in Britain was stressed to me by a shoe shop proprietor I met in North Africa. He told me that he had placed an order with a British firm which they took six months to deliver.

'That was a long time,' I observed, expecting to hear about how Patagonian shoes could be had within six hours, or something of the sort. I am rather used to being told such tales of woe when travelling and incautious enough to say that I lived in the United Kingdom.

But no; this time it was even more strange. 'The matter, O my brother,' said the Berber, 'is curious, and bears repetition. Perhaps you can even shed some light upon it.'

'Pray recite the entire narrative,' I responded. 'And for your confidence, I thank you.'

'Thank me not – it is my duty,' he replied, and this is his tale:

'I ordered the shoes in January. They arrived in July. When I examined one of them, I found in it the photograph of a young girl and a note in English. She gave an address in Northampton, England, and wrote that she was a packer in a shoe factory, and unmarried. She would like to meet a man with his own business, perhaps a shoe shop, with a view to matrimony. She was, she said, twenty years of age.'

'How romantic!' I said, as my interlocutor paused with his beady eyes fixed on me. 'What did you do? Wrote to her, I suppose?'

'Better than that,' replied my friend; 'I decided to surprise her, for her beauty had enraptured my heart. I bought valuable presents and hied me forth, to Northampton. I went by aircraft and then by bus.'

'And you met her?'

'Patience, my friend, haste is from the Devil.'

I composed myself as best I could. By now we had installed ourselves at a table in the café next door to the shoe shop, so I covered my diabolical impatience by swallowing a gulp of mint tea.

'I journeyed, as I have told you, to that big town in the north of England mentioned in the damsel's note. I found the street, then the house, known by its number, as many are in those parts. Then I rang the doorbell.

'A fat, middle-aged woman opened the door. I told her that I had come to see the maiden whose name I had memorised, and whose photograph I thrust towards her.

'I added that, as the mother or other senior member of her household, she could be assured that my attentions were honourable, and that I would only see the maiden chaperoned.'

He heaved a great sigh.

'But did you get to see her?' Again I could not restrain myself.

He sighed again. 'Alas! She invited me in, and told me to sit down. She was laughing so that she could hardly speak. She said something very rapidly to a great hairy savage of a man who came into the room. Then he, too, laughed.

'Now she spoke. Slowly, because she realised I didn't
understand their local dialect too well. She said: "Bless you, love!
That note and that picture were *ME*! But that were all done
twenty-five years ago. I've been married these twenty years, and
I have three grown-up children ... Those shoes didn't sell too
quickly, did they? Where did you say you came from?"'

'She had never heard of North Africa, and I'd never heard
of brown ale, which they tried to make me drink. Verily, England
is a land of magic and mystery.'

A sad, if romantic, tale, indeed. Eager to collect information
for this book, I asked Sidi Ali what else had happened to him
in England.

'Very little,' he said, 'because I returned here as fast as I could,
and also because my English was rather weak.

'So weak, indeed, that I think a bus conductor in London
imagined that I wanted to collect fifty-pence pieces.'

'How so?'

'Well, I had only a £50 note, and I said to this man when he
came to sell me a ticket for fifty pence — in my best English,
of course — I am sorry, I have no 50-pence coin."

'He immediately replied: "Don't worry about that. You'll soon
have 99 of them!" and he gave me the entire change in those
coins ... What should I have said?'

'Nothing,' I answered, 'in my experience, would have been
much use in the circumstances.'

'Well, at least,' said the Berber, 'people are kind to you in
England. They just seem a little late in commercial deliveries and
in not always understanding your needs. I believe that our
commerce, here in the *souq*, moves faster.'

Obviously, it is not necessary to have a special technique when
applying the slowness factor internationally: just behave to
foreigners as you do to each other.

Of course, nothing in England is quite what it appears on the
surface. I have often observed that everything here is for a reason
— one only has to seek diligently enough to find it. So, how does
the English reputation for fair play, and just plain niceness fit
in with Masterly Inactivity, or even laziness?

Geoffrey Wheatcroft,[1] speaks of English niceness as 'a
myth'. The English upper classes, he says, notoriously disarm
their victims with charm before entrapping or defrauding them.

They are sometimes termed 'attractively lazy', he says, but 'the paralytic sloth of the English goes hand in hand with an envenomed resentment of anyone . . . who chooses to do some work.'

The myth of English niceness, he says, is central to the 'great English confidence trick.'

How is that performed? Well, 'Having first persuaded ourselves, we then persuaded the rest of the world that we had invented and copyrighted decency, honesty and fair play.'

Niceness, according to Mr. Wheatcroft, is the lower-class version of the upper-class charm.

Since we could not really call Mr. Wheatcroft's article nice (and therefore lower-class), perhaps he is to be seen as a member of the upper classes. On the other hand, reading him again, I cannot discern much (upper-class) charm, either. Possibly, then, he is middle-class.

In any case, he can observe his fellow-countrymen in a way that no foreigner would perhaps dare, though he does not seem to be able to explain them. Indeed, his last sentence asks, in a very English manner, 'how do we do it?'

The British educational system has traditionally been designed to instil a sound sense of Masterly Inactivity into students. In times past, the English tried to make foreign-born 'natives' into little Brits, by sending them to study at Harrow, Sandhurst and so on, hoping to use them in due course as surrogate rulers. Note what David Martin says of this, in his *General Amin*[2]:

> With the death of Kabaka Daudi Chwa in 1939, his son Mutesa II became Kabaka at the age of fifteen. During the forties he spent about four years in Britain, first at Cambridge University, and later in the Grenadier Guards, where King George VI gave him a commission as a captain. It was a period which moulded his life, making him the most inept Kabaka in memory.

Things have, indeed, changed. That a British education might actually make someone unfit to rule his own people was unthinkable to generations of colonial administrators and the like.

Of course, what seems to be delay or procrastination to the foreigner may only be the result of a faulty − or insufficiently English − education on his part. A friend did not get his grazed hand attended to at the casualty department of a London hospital because he couldn't answer a simple question.

He knew English pretty well, too. But when he was unable to reply or even understand the casualty officer's increasingly irate enquiry, he turned tail and fled.

He arrived at my door shortly afterwards. 'In my country,' he said, 'they would have looked at the wound and dressed it. This man had to have the answer, and wouldn't do a thing until I satisfied him on this very difficult query; really technical it was, and I'm no doctor . . .'

'What were the exact words?' I thought he would surely have remembered, or written them down. After all, he did know a lot of English — we were using it at the time.

'It was too difficult. Amazing words, I tell you.'

I cleaned and dressed his graze myself with the help of the first-aid box, and hastened to the scene of his discomfiture, a major teaching hospital in London.

It took a bit of doing, as you can imagine, but eventually I managed to see the physician who had tried to treat my friend. I explained that I was helping him with his English and wanted to know the exact form of words that had been used in connection with the grazed hand.

He was quite co-operative; people in London are in general kindly about foreigners and their difficulties. 'Yes, I remember the case well. Couldn't have been more than a couple of hours ago. Discharged himself before treatment.'

'What was his difficulty?'

'Very poor English. He'd slipped and fallen over, had an abrasion on one palm. I merely asked him "Have you determined the presence or otherwise of particulate matter?" and he asked me to say it again. Repeated it three of four times, actually.'

'Of course, you meant "Do you know if there is anything in the cut?"'

'Exactly.'

This particular British attitude — a combination of confidence and carelessness — may help explain how they were able to dominate so much of the world during their Empire. Today the Empire is gone, but the attitude remains.

I was at the Departures area at Heathrow Airport not so long ago, among a huge crowd waiting for a flight to West Africa.

There were only two white men among the intending passengers. The pilot of the aircraft, followed by members of his crew, appeared and started to weave through the throng when one of the Englishmen stopped him.

'I say, Captain,' he giggled, 'this one will kill you! I'm seeing my friend off, and I've been telling him that if he's captured by cannibals in your country — he's not to get into too much of a stew!'

They say the Devil has the best tunes. As to the best jokes between the British and foreigners ...

Of course, we foreigners cannot always be certain that we have grasped the point of English jokes. My late father recited an anecdote related to him by an African Head of State when the former was Indian cultural envoy to West Asia.

The story went that there was a certain British lord who was with a visiting commercial mission. He was only there to give some tone to the group because his title looked good on the letter-paper of a large English company. Otherwise, he was rather unimpressed by 'trade' as his people called it.

During a reception in the Third World country, someone approached the Peer and offered him a visiting-card. 'My business card,' he said.

'Ah, yes,' said the noble Lord; 'I have seen one of these before. In fact my grandmother once had one. Borrowed it, of course. But then, she *was* a gipsy, they say ...'

This narrative always had people in stitches of laughter. After telling it for some years, just to make sure that I understood it, I asked a retired British ambassador what he thought of it.

'Excellent!' he said.

Then he elucidated. 'You see, the Peer was being polite without selling out his own principles. Also, by referring to his rather ordinary ancestry, he was able to relate to the man he was talking to. He must have been briefed that the man with the card was a nomad, or something. Our chaps on the spot are rather good at that sort of thing, you know ...'

And, of course, it is okay in England to have a grandmother who was a gipsy or actress, but not a father or mother who was one.

Things, though, are changing fast. A leader in the *Evening Standard* picked up the trend offered by the noble Lord:

The Princess Royal urges an end to discrimination against gipsies. She says this is caused by ignorance about their lifestyles. Gipsies like to travel, dislike conventional jobs, are expert horse-copers and hold mystical beliefs. Just like another group whom she may have been subconsciously defending: the Royal Family.[3]

And many people, indeed, openly boast of ancestors hanged for sheep-stealing. Not too recent an ancestor, though.

8

Teapoys and Boiled Potatoes

'I was once giving a lecture in England, when
somebody stood up and contradicted me. The
chairman rubbed his hands with delight. "This
is fine," he said, "now we can have a good
row".'

– General Sir John Glubb,
My Years with the Arabs[1]

Glubb Pasha is speaking here, in a most absorbing monograph,
of the consensual and non-adversarial nature of Arabian society,
and contrasting it with the habit of controversy which is so highly
valued in the West.

The Arabs are a highly articulate people, and this perhaps
prepared them for the inevitable cultural clash with Westerners
in the past (the Crusades), with the European imperialists – and
for the confrontations caused by today's shrinking world.

This latter, far from making us all brothers, realising that we
are all in this thing together, and so on – the formula so beloved
of the idealists – could have the reverse effect.

As peoples are thrown almost instantly together, they note each
other's peculiarities too rapidly for smooth convergence. Friction
increases everywhere. As always, optimists, like pessimists, leave
something out of their calculations.

There was an instructive reaction to something I wrote in
Darkest England at the point where the Arab Sheikh Anwar is
railing against the English phrasebook *Say it in Arabic!* This book
purports to be a guide to Arabic, but is far from lacking in
blunders and absurdities.

A few Arabs decided that I was making fun of their people,
and even demanded the book's withdrawal. Others, however,

from similar backgrounds, asked me for more. Three British people – they actually signed their letters – accused me of 'putting forth a stereotype of comfort only to Zionists.'

One correspondent claimed that it is not politically correct to laugh at people of 'any other preference, race, tribe, persuasion, type, kind, gender, sex or tendency.' At least she seems to be getting full value from her *Roget's Thesaurus*.

Now, not many months after *Darkest England* was published, I received, anonymously, a copy of another book designed to teach Arabic to English-speakers. An unsigned note, in block letters was tucked inside. It said: 'YOU AIN'T SEEN NOTHING YET!'

I settled in my comfortable library chair to possess myself of the book's wisdom: but the more I tried to understand it, the more confused I became.

I read it through several times, struggling with the text far into the night, trying to discover why it had been written, for whom, and how. More importantly, what did it really *mean*? I remained baffled.

My thoughts drifted to the earlier self-teaching book on this subject, which had given such perplexity to so many. Many Arabs had told me they were delighted with my chapter about it in *Darkest England*. Not least Sheikh Anwar al Agali: who was sure that the extraordinary booklet was in code. Perhaps my anonymous correspondent had sent him a copy of this new volume – because it wasn't long before I was holding in my hand a fax from the Sheikh. Freely translated, his excellent calligraphy said:

My dear brother: Peace upon thee! God willing
You are well, all is well with you, you are
Satisfied and a thousand welcomes ...

But afterwards: Thou may'st recall the time
When, at your home in Inglaterra we spoke of
Hawks and camels and finally I disclosed my
Suspicions about a book purporting to teach
Arabic to Britanavi infidels.

I was, and am, convinced, that it is a plot
Of a deep and continuing nature, designed

To conceal unworthy intentions.
Or an abomination of some other kind.

The proof of this I shall bring with me
To Londra when I shall, insh'Allah, show this
Disgraceful object to you.

I agree that you were wise, on reflection,
To reserve judgment in this earlier matter, when you
Indicated, though subtly and politely,
That you were not convinced of the plot,
But rather of the ignorance of the compilers.
Now you will see the facts, plainly.
And upon thee blessings!

I, of course, immediately faxed back, in appropriate terms:

Hadir! [I am present!]:
May thy days be long! Head, eyes and heart are
At thy service, as always. Welcomes without
Limit to my tents. For bringing
So much light into an otherwise dull existence,
A thousand thanks.

A stickler for etiquette as always, the Sheikh acknowledged
this with:

There is no [reason to] thank [me]: it is my duty.

Which was very civil of him.

It seemed no time at all before the telephone rang, the security
men had swept through the house, (to take up positions
surrounding it); the rugs and cushions were laid, the music, food
and coffee arranged. Al Agali appeared, fierce beard, gold-
embroidered flowing brown robes (made from the cloth of the
soft hair of the finest camels of Kuwait), curved, silver-sheathed
disembowelling knife and all.

'*Awwal ta'am, wa baduhu kalam,* first food, after that talk,'
I said: and we ate. Four minutes in the microwave, and the frozen
palau was perfect.

After the second cup of coffee (the third means, of course,
'go home') Sheikh Anwar produced his copy of, yes, the second
of these contentious books on Arabic for the English.

I had not mentioned the matter, being unwilling to steal his thunder. Few things would have been more discourteous in Arabian circles than to say, 'I have a copy, too.'

The book looked promising enough from the outside, as I had already noted. Did it not carry the imprimatur of the Oxford University Press? With that cachet, it would surely sell well: especially to those who wanted *A Course in Spoken Arabic*.[2]

Oxford University: one of the great centres of learning of the Western world. I said as much to the Sheikh, who snorted.

'The more pretentious the goat, the more mangy it is! And the higher up-river it drinks, polluting the stream!' he roared.

He looked at me expectantly. It was my turn, so I supplied: '*Kull anzah yataaruf gati'aha,* every goat knows her own herd.'

'Exactly,' said the Sheikh; 'and, if this is a product of the English university herd, its fellows, even those abroad, will know it by its quality. The quality here being in doubt, what is amiss, I ask you?'

He continued, '*Kathir al-ayadi tahrig at-taam,* many hands will burn the food — you have a look for yourself.'

There were markers, bits of feebly-adhesive paper, in that curious pale yellow affected by American lawyers and others, adhering to certain pages of the *Course*. I looked at the first, marking page 18.

The Sheikh was sitting close by, his unblinking black eyes fixed on me, his shoulders heaving as he tried to conceal his excitement.

'Yes, yes! Read it to me ...'

I obeyed:

"'Translate into English:

1   Two cooks   2   Two months
3   Two days   4   Two tailors
5   Two pens.''

'But these are *already* in English!' I cried, once more confused and feeling rather odd.

'Precisely,' said Agali. His English had improved immensely since our adventures in the English countryside, when I had, perforce, been his interpreter at Badgersden village fête. 'Now you may try another page.'

I soon came across a *tarazezeh*, which I had never heard of before. 'Neither have I!' rumbled the Sheikh; 'and, what is more, they actually say that this word, which is not Arabic as I know it, is in English *A Teapoy!*'

He recited from the text: 'Throw a stone into this walnut tree, will you?'

'Sounds pretty rum to me,' I said, matching his proverb (as he had a right to expect) with another. I chose: 'I feel like a Monday in the middle of the week'.

The Sheikh was looking even more serious. 'If Oxford University is teaching Arabic like this, no wonder Eastern audiences so often roar with laughter at the BBC, thinking that people are telling obscure jokes during the news.'

'But what,' continued the Sheikh, 'What *is* a Teapoy? It says here that it is an English word. Even if they don't know any Arabic at the Oxford University Press, at least they must know what a Teapoy is.'

He fixed me with that look which I get from my fellow-Easterners when they think, as they often do, that I know nothing about Britain or the English language. Usually when I am trying to explain some anomaly.

I said, 'I am not really a philologist, you know, brother, and I may not know the exact meaning of this apparently English word . . .'

He interrupted me: 'I know thy lineage, and it is a long, honourable and distinguished one. But if thou art about to plead that your ancestors are *Sharifs*, not men of the pen, remember one thing. Thy lineal ancestor, the Holy Prophet (Upon whom prayers and the Salute!) was illiterate, that is well known. But *Thou* art not a prophet!'

'Perish the thought!' I exclaimed, 'but we always remember the adage: *Alas! alas!,* the root [of all] *is* pedigree . . .'

'O Sayed!' grated the Sheikh, 'more appropriate, surely is the saying "*Inna kunt Sayed, la taziyid*", even if a lord behave not in lordly fashion.'

He put the boot in with: '*Aslak fi fa'lak* – Thy pedigree is [best seen] in thy actions.'

I couldn't think of a quotation to cap that one, so I decided to come clean.

'I am sorry, O Sheikh! I have never heard of a teapoy.'

'Bring a dictionary, then, an *English* one,' he spat. But I refused to do this, for fear of losing face, until I had rung, in the Sheikh's presence, several English friends, including philologists, to see if they could tell me the meaning of the English word which the so-erudite Oxford people had included. Surely, if they were doing a colloquial guide, this word should be colloquial? Not one of the people I canvassed had the faintest idea.

Finally, however, we tracked teapoy down. It is a bastard-Persian/English word, used in India from the early nineteenth century, to describe a three-legged table, a sort of tripod. (Later, my sister, Amina, seldom stumped, recalled that.)

I suddenly realised, then, that what Oxford thought was *Tarazezah*, was really *Tarabezah,* a table — not a three-legged one at all.

'There are other mysteries,' the Sheikh assured me, 'which make me suspect that all this is something to do with British Intelligence.'

Ignoring my remark that the last person I'd met who'd been in touch with British Intelligence swore that this was 'a contradiction in terms', the Sheikh grabbed the book and showed me first page 69 and then page 73.

'These unbelievers are up to something: you may count on it. There is a reference here to post offices which simply does not, cannot, make sense. I think it is to do with some kind of secret rendezvous.'

It certainly looked curious. The first extract gave a phrase which might have meant 'Where is the Post Office?' — in a mishmash of colloquial and literary Arabic words.

However, all seemed fair so far: our student is looking for the Post Office. But even when he has found it (I know that he has done so because the book says 'At the Post Office') he still insists on asking: 'Where is the Post Office?'

'There is another explanation,' said the Sheikh. 'Perhaps they are all mad. Look at this one: "Is there a train for Delhi?" Not only is there no train for Delhi, but there is no conceivable possibility that, if you ask anyone in Arabic for a train to Delhi, he will understand you. Delhi simply is not connected to any railway where Arabic is spoken.

'Of course, the whole thing could be a joke; but I don't think so. I feel something amiss in my bones: *Al galb shahid,* the heart is witness.'

He continued, probably to maintain the flow of sayings which characterizes polite conversation in his circle: 'This book is like the Mill of the Jinn: rumbling and clinking — and producing no flour!'

I had to agree with him. I had just come across the phrase: 'I work with Gopaldas & Co.' There may be no doubt that Gopaldas is a firm of the highest repute and greatest probity and importance. But this is a thoroughly Hindu, Hindi-Sanskrit name, and less likely to be found in an Arab country than Wilberforce-Fotheringay-Bloggs. Furthermore, this particular employee earns 'Rupees nine hundred per month.'

Rupees? Well, I suppose Gopaldas *could* pay salaries in rupees, but I can't see any Arab — or Englishman or American for that matter — being too pleased with that.

It is probably illegal as well: for you cannot export rupees willy nilly (and you certainly could not in 1978, when Oxford gave this great work to the world).

Of course, our hero might have been trying to get to Delhi to get his rupees there from Messrs. Gopaldas. It seems unlikely, though — even if he had agreed to take his pay in such an unusual currency — that he would ever receive it.

I say this because he is evidently so dim that I wouldn't blame Mr. Gopaldas for firing him in under a month, tarazezah, teapoy and all.

A man who wants a train to Delhi, asking in Arabic — presumably intent on writing or wiring Gopaldas to have his money ready — gets to the Post Office and cannot recognise it: that's what we are dealing with.

And he'd have to travel from Arabia to Delhi, deal with Gopaldas, and return, all on £12.33 which is about what Rupees 900 is worth.

There is a lighter moment, of course. This is when our hero the learner, perhaps after trying to change the rupees which are not convertible, at least has a use for his teapoy. He says, in passable Arabic: 'Bring me boiled potatoes.' Not curry, not goat-and-rice, but the food that all Easterners imagine is the staple in England: boiled potatoes.

He obviously isn't a progressive: we can infer that much about him. It cannot be politically correct to order such DWEM (politically correct for dead-white-European-male) dishes in the East.

It should have been, at the least, vegetarian curry (to carry on the Indian motif) or 'stew without goat, please'. Of course, under stress, people do revert to type: and the poor man perhaps did need a rapid injection of boiled potatoes, just to restore his morale.

I did not submit entirely to the Arab Sheikh's belief in a deep-laid plot by infidels. Nor did I yield to the temptation to believe that Oxford University Press needs its head examined (and, possibly, some consistent and correct Arabic inserted). But I remained puzzled.

I still wasn't much more enlightened when I woke up, cold and stiff, in my library chair, with the clock showing three o'clock in the morning − and the list of all those amazing passages neatly written out in my handwriting on a clipboard pad. Not refreshed by my fitful sleep, still worrying: and depressed to find that the Sheikh was still at home, among his camels and palm-trees . . .

9

Say It Loud Enough And They Won't Believe It . . .

'On the one hand, we never shall be slaves and we swear we won't bow the knee to any living foreigner. On the other hand, we are quite happy to grovel to the German family we pay to adorn our stamps.'
— Kate Saunders, *The Sunday Times*[1]

I once asked an English nobleman who had been a government Minister why the Brits ran themselves down so much, both in conversation and in the Press.

'Simple, my dear chap,' he said. 'It's because of the EAP Factor.'

This turned out to be the Edgar Allen Poe Factor: named after Poe's story, *The Purloined Letter*[2], in which a missing envelope was not found because it was in the most obvious place — a letter-rack.

What the English (and their British imitators) do, he explained, is follow the Aesopian teaching: shout things loud and often from the rooftops — having discovered that then nobody will believe them.

I wondered how, in that case, advertising could work in England. Companies spent fortunes every day trying to outshout one another about everything from margarine to moth-killers. Not to mention the British boasts — among other things — that they have the world's oldest and most democratic parliament, the best legal system, are located in the temperate zone and enjoy better hygiene than anyone else. The world has believed them. It still largely does, in fact, though the British are now — in their currently favourite phrase – doing a U-turn on these and many other things.

No, I am afraid that this must remain a mystery. The best that the observer can do At This Moment In Time (favourite English cliché: what other moments are there, apart from those in time?) is to record a process, make notes, examine data.

Readers of my previous books on the Island Race will recall that I have alluded to some suspected hidden hand or Group Mind which inspires, even controls, the way in which the community moves. Ephemeral though it may be, this concept is well worth keeping in mind as we continue our investigations.

The likely existence of this shadowy element in a broad range of activities suggests it is constantly trying to diffuse its shifting principles, practices and presence throughout the populace. If this is the case, this book, dedicated to spreading the understanding of Englishry, must play a part.

The idea of obedience to the secret, almost unperceived Group Mind is beguiling indeed: the more so the further one pursues it. If you ask British people what nationality they feel themselves to be, as likely as not they will answer 'Nothing really.'

What about people from other countries? What are they? 'Oh, they're foreigners' is the most usual reply. Now, where does this unanimity of attitude come from, if not from a Group Mind? Nobody teaches it openly, surely?

One strongly cherished idea here is that English people don't think about themselves. Very well: but in that case how is it that, in my thirty-year collection of Press cuttings on a diverse range of subjects, those marked 'England and the English' from British newspapers are twenty times as numerous as any other category?

The English, it seems are obsessed with themselves, while at the same time remaining quite unaware of this preoccupation. Where did the prompting for *that* come from?

It is interesting to note that brutish behaviour among the British is quite often equated with lower-class origins. Thus Professor Richard Layard, of the London School of Economics, which has no particular reputation for right wing views:

Britain has a lumpen proletariat unlike any other advanced

nation and this shows not only in British factories but on football terraces around the world.[3]

For my money, the lumpen behaviour I've often observed displayed by otherwise cultivated people suggests the tendency suffuses the whole population, not just an unpopular section of it. But are these people really being instructed by the Group Mind how to behave and what to say? Examples of what — to the foreigner — may seem like brutish insensitivity — may be heard every day.

For instance, only yesterday, at an otherwise glittering social occasion, I overheard an Englishman's opening conversational gambit: 'So you're a vegetarian, eh? Well, you know what they say: nothing wrong with vegetarianism that a good steak wouldn't cure.'

In today's paper, moreover, I see that English people are given advice about how to treat the natives when visiting France. They should praise food, children and so on. They should not say that they don't appreciate wine. And, if you please, they shouldn't say that they are glad to note that the French drains have been improved, or that the weather is better in some terribly windswept part of the United Kingdom.

It must be remembered that the English (and British) attitude towards foreigners is exactly the same behaviour the British extend towards one another.

I was sitting at an informal outdoor meal once when a very English lady, of undeniably good background, said casually in conversation to her vis-à-vis (who was wearing a roll neck sweater): 'I do dislike those roll neck sweaters, don't you?' They were both English people. The culprit did not seem at all taken aback, I was glad to note, and merely answered with a scowl.

Rather more disconcerted, at a dinner-party I attended, was a poor Scandinavian ambassador. His aristocratic hostess fixed him with an interested stare and said in the conversational tone customary at table: 'Did you know it is *extremely* unlucky to have one brown and one blue eye?'

As it happened, his Excellency did have one eye of each colour; and all his years of diplomatic service could not prevent him from looking highly discomposed by the very English remark by the very English duchess.

There is a lot of talk, too, about the difference between the Celtic Fringe peoples — the Irish, Scots, Welsh, Manx, Cornish — and the English. Careful examination shows, however, that although the Celts often speak of the English as a different — sometimes very different — people, they tend to behave and especially to write in their newspapers in very much the same way. The English way, what else? Why don't they know this? Is it anything to do with what Peter McKay claims is: 'the unrivalled British talent for self-delusion and humbug'?[4] As I am not British, I am given to looking for a general theory to account for almost anything English. My non-English readers expect as much. And even the English, to whom this book is primarily addressed, may appreciate at least some guidelines other than those obtained from their social environment. My unsolicited contribution, I know, will be welcome — if only because the English have lapped up two books like this already — and also because they diligently reprint in the daily Press anything they can find about themselves. My cuttings file on the British is only rivalled by the one which concerns the alleged iniquities of the French.

Now, what general theory, I wondered, could link such things as the unexpectedness of the Edgar Allen Poe or EAP Factor and the niceness which isn't; the U-turn of boasting and humility; and the self-obsession of the newspaper cuttings with the belief that English people are unaware of belonging to any particular nationality?

It took a bit of doing, but at length I trapped the outline of a General Theory. Alongside the concept of the Group Mind must be set the ambiguous raised almost to an art-form. A deliberate determination not to be specific, to a degree that elsewhere only the Chinese are reported to have attained.

This particular form of chaos is categorised by its practitioners in a special phrase, music to British ears but enraging to a greater or lesser degree to anyone else, according to the circumstances. That phrase is: Muddling Through.

For me, the moment of illumination came when I learned something that would lift the heart of any self-respecting psychiatrist faced with an English person. Old English, say the authorities, had no word for 'tomorrow'. What *could* one do but muddle through?

Those who have themselves been muddled by the process should take comfort from the fact that this is not intended. The individual is never the target. After all, almost by definition, the person Muddling Through doesn't see clearly that he is doing it. Or he may defend it and call it something entirely different. Listen to Chris Patten, at the time he was Minister for Overseas Development:

> 'Periodic attempts to replace our generous and instinctive pragmatism and the clutter it occasionally creates, with something more efficient, all of an ideological piece, come to very little. This should neither surprise nor disturb us.'[5]

Take an everyday example: when you enter a shop, an assistant may well approach you with the phrase: 'Can I help you?' – apparently believing that he or she is there for that purpose. In reality, of course, it is at least equally you who are there to help the assistant to earn a living. Not to mention helping the shop, helping commerce as a whole, helping the taxman, and so on.

Similarly, people constantly write letters to their customers begging them 'not to hesitate' to seek information, clarification and so on. Now, why on earth should anyone hesitate if in contact with a firm for some purpose of mutual interest or concern? Only an English person might be able to tell you. Except that the Group Mind is too busy muddling through to carry out exercises of this kind.

It is, too, only in England that commercial firms refer to *themselves* as 'Messrs'. Of course, the correct form is to style yourself 'Bloggs and Co.', and let your correspondent, customer or whoever, add the honorific 'Messrs'. But, in England, wholly respectable firms do it.

Even my chimney-sweep, when first calling at the house, gave tongue with: 'Name o' Shaar? I'm Mister Smith.'

A great deal of this has to do with the language. It is so vague that one sometimes wonders whether it could be vaguer. I heartily agree with the Oxford don whom I've just been hearing on the radio, vociferously claiming that English is so marvellous that it will forever remain unplumbed.

Immediately following this very touching encomium, I dropped in at my local pharmacy for some pills I'd been prescribed. The Indian chemist was almost beside himself with rage.

'This language, this English, is positively dangerous!' he was saying. 'The instructions plainly are: "Take one twice a day". Now, this is physically impossible. Once you have taken one, you have taken it. You CAN only take it once! To take one and the same pill twice a day would require an internal operation. Where would that get you, eh?'

I must ask him, sometime, how to take another kind of tablet I have been prescribed. Not only has this to be taken three times a day, but for five days *running*.

This, of course, comes under a similar heading to phrases already dealt with, such as DOGS MUST BE CARRIED ON THE ESCALATOR, and CHECK CONTENTS OF THIS WAGE-PACKET BEFORE OPENING. It is generally believed by my research department, pending further investigation, that these terms have been invented by that same special area of the Group Mind which issues those road-signs, all over the country, which point nowhere, contradict each other, or simply peter out, just when you need them most.

For years I wondered how, if it were the Group Mind at work, the signposts and such things as English idioms arrived at any consensus at all. Then I saw the answer, in an article by Vernon Bogdanor, reader in Government at Oxford University, though admittedly not in a precisely similar context:

As one constitutional authority declared at the beginning of the century: 'We live under a system of tacit understandings. But the understandings are often misunderstood'.[6]

Anything more deliciously muddling-through would, surely, be hard to find? *The Observer,* where the article appears, certainly got the point: for the distinguished Fellow of Brasenose College's article was appropriately titled MAKING IT UP AS WE GO ALONG.

Even better was done by one British government minister who was entertaining a visiting overseas dignitary in London. Have you ever wondered, when watching TV news, what all the delegates are laughing at when the cameras are allowed in, just for a peep, before they get down to work at some high-level international conference? Well, here is your chance to learn: they tell jokes.

The event I was present at was one such 'summit'-type get-together. The Minister was seated beside an envoy who had been, some years before, labelled a notorious terrorist. Today he was a senior statesman in a respectable country not a thousand miles from the Middle East.

Apparently determined to twist any part of the lion's tail he could get hold of, the visitor remarked how the British had always claimed that they never wanted an empire, but that it had come about by chance. It was not their fault.

'Ah', said the British host, 'I can give you an analogy. It is in a tale I heard recently.'

We settled down to listen, in the dead time while conference details were being arranged: and this was the gist of it:

A hungry and thirsty man was once trudging to his capital city in a certain Middle Eastern country. He flagged down car after car, whizzing along the dusty highway. But even if they stopped, the drivers refused to listen to him when they realised, from his appeals, that he was only a poor local farmer. After a time, he tried to experiment. When the next car stopped, he claimed to be – an Englishman.

Great was his delight when the driver motioned him into the passenger seat. But suddenly the driver stopped at a melon-field, pulled out a gun and ordered his terrified passenger to steal a melon.

The poor man obeyed, and the driver grinned. 'I stole this car,' he said, 'and I'm escaping the police in it. I needed refreshment. I'll kill you in a moment. What have you got to say for yourself, infidel scum?'

'Only this,' replied the poor man. 'I have been an Englishman for less than an hour, and already I'm a liar and a thief.'

There was an enormous roar of laughter at this, which enabled the television commentator to say, 'The delegates seemed to be in the very best of spirits, which augurs well for the Conference'. You can hardly blame him, since it would have been regarded as poor TV indeed if he had simply repeated the joke, which he probably hadn't heard anyway. Our Political/Middle East/UN/East Asia, etc., Correspondent is seldom actually present at such events, and is merely shoved into a room with an editing apparatus and told to produce a commentary and a few significant sound-bites for the News.

Of course, the top guest — the former terrorist — had also brought his own joke with which to hit the conference. The talk among the aides beforehand had been that his contribution would easily prevail over anything the British were likely to produce. He told it during the banquet which followed the confabulations, and was plainly confident that it would be a knockout. Here it is:

> Not so very long ago, and certainly when they had a price on my head, as it were, it was said that the British Empire was one on which the sun never set — because the Almighty couldn't trust you people in the dark! I toast you just the same!

Somehow, however, this sally did not get one-quarter the applause which had greeted the English Minister's one against his own people. And the visiting big shot was discernibly no chess player: for he gave the Englishman a chance to come back with another, but equally effective, self-deprecating one:

> 'Your Excellency has been kind enough to refer to our supposedly diminished role since the Empire was transformed into our proud Commonwealth. Naturally, many things have changed. And, if indeed we were not trusted when the sun did not set on us, must we not take it as a compliment from Heaven that, empireless, we are therefore now obviously trusted in the dark with the rest of you?'

Well, at least you now have a fly-on-the-wall picture of the vital matters discussed at international conferences.

10

Travelling, Visiting, Empiring

'Bivouacking on a spur of the Black Mountain
(22 October 1888) the Seaforths lighted a
roaring camp fire round which we sang and
danced reels and played the pipes. One
Highland Fling was danced on a Hassanzai
gravestone! ... on the 30th, the Hassanzais
paid their fine and brought in their last
remaining prisoner, so the War may now be
considered as over.'

– *The Life and Times of*
Lieut.-General Sir James Moncreiffe[1]

One of the battles, the small wars, against the Afghan clans of
the Frontier was, indeed, over. But, as my friend the great
Professor Majrooh of Kabul put it, 'one of the advanced customs
of the West – dancing on the opponent's gravestones – never
somehow took with the uncivilised Afghans'. Even when they
later saw the British, and still later the Russians, off their premises.

There are dozens of good, perhaps true, stories about the
Afghan Pashtun people and their contact with the British when
the latter pushed up to – and sometimes through – the Khyber
Pass in the belief that the Russians might appear at any moment
and attack India. Failure to do this despite all the prodigies of
effort and suffering it involved would, they were convinced, result
in the loss of India.

The Pashtuns were, and still are to a large extent, a law unto
themselves. Probably the world's very finest fighting men, even
the British couldn't stop them carrying, stealing, importing and
making arms, travelling free on the railways, and generally
behaving in a disorderly manner.

They also love money: and some of their chiefs are extremely rich men; though they have their ups and downs. They tell of a Pashtun who visited a British bank in the North-West Frontier area, and asked the manager for a loan. 'What security have you?' The Pashtun opened his furlined jacket and showed a gold belt, encrusted with diamonds and rubies. Some months later, the borrower returned to pay his debt, peeling the sum off a huge roll of dollar bills. The manager was interested:

'Why don't you let me look after that for you?' The Pashtun grinned. 'First let me see your belt,' he said.

Although the Afghans have often been at war with the Brits, astonishingly no rancour remains between the two peoples. For decades, according to the Afghan Professor, 'Afghans were sewn into pigskins to dissuade them from opposing the would-be conquering British Army. Kabul, the Afghan capital, was the first undefended civilian city to be attacked from the air — by the RAF. Still no enmity.'

I put it down to the fact that the British have so many endearing qualities that the rest of us really like them, in spite of activities, from time to time, which the Brits themselves frequently label as not quite acceptable in others. Once you have known some of them, you can't really hate them, can you? Whatever they might have done or what you have read of their exploits.

Mind you, there seem to be many among the Brits who feel deeply about these things: perhaps more deeply than the victims. When I quoted Churchill as claiming to be from a community of 'reformed pirates' I was assailed by a storm of letters from British people. Ninety-nine per cent of them were enraged beyond temperance. They claimed that atrocities and crimes must never be allowed to be forgotten. They said that the treatment of the black slaves from Africa by the British; of the Kurds, poison-gassed by the same; of the Chinese, by the British opium lords; of the Boers; of the Indians massacred on General Dyer's orders: these and several others were crimes that cried out for eternal remembrance and compensation.

Lord Moyne, whom I'd always found to be the gentlest of souls, took me to his London house and harangued me for an hour about these and other atrocities — plying me the while with glasses of sweet redcurrant juice and water.

I don't know about the others, but Dyer, like a good many other soldiers, does seem to have lost his nerve. However, the military can't always be all bad, even during empiring. Take the matter of the English officers on Minorca and the elopement of the disenchanted nuns, which I abridge here:

MINORCA [goes the account in *Anecdotiana*, published in London in 1841] is an island in the Mediterranean; alternately possessed by England and Spain; for a long time gallantly defended, in the 18th century, against forces enormously superior to his own by General Blakeney.

Speaking of the celebrated siege of Fort St. Philip, the intrepid veteran used to relate an incident previous to it which perplexed him as much as the enemy's attacks. This was the elopement of three nuns [in 1748] from the monastery of St. Claire with two English officers. These gentlemen, induced by curiosity to converse at the iron grate, saw two of the fair recluses: with whom they fell desperately in love and declared their passion; solemnly promising at the same time to marry them, if they could contrive to escape from their confinement.

The military men soon found that their offers were by no means disagreeable, and many schemes were formed by the prisoners to elude the vigilance of their keepers.

At length, by one of those happy accidents to which lovers as well as warriors are sometimes indebted for success, they procured the key of a door from the house into an adjoining garden.

Taking advantage of darkness and the extreme age of the nun whose business it was to lock them up, at midnight they crept softly downstairs into the garden, where they found the two gentlemen ready to receive them. The lovers were surprised and abashed when a *third* lady made her appearance, but their apprehensions were soon quieted on being informed that the stranger was an intimate friend and confidante who, hating her captivity and dreading a deprivation of their society, had insisted on accompanying them.

There yet remained a considerable difficulty to surmount: this was a wall twenty feet high which surrounded the garden of the convent on every side. To men with rope-ladders, who were resolved to run all risks to gain possession of youth and beauty, this seemed nothing. But to girls, neither of whom had reached the age of nineteen, the attempt was formidable: besides the risk of being heard or seen or persons passing in the street where they were to descend.

By a concurrence of caution and good luck the nuns climbed safely over the wall and were lodged by the fortunate lovers in safe and creditable quarters.

The next day, at early matins, when the fugitives were missed, the town as well as the convent became a scene of uproar and confusion. The English were strongly suspected of assisting in this escape: the inhabitants, for the most part rigid Catholics, being sure that none but heretics could be capable of so wicked and abominable an action.

The officers, in the meantime, applied to their chaplain to marry them according to the rites of the Church of England.

This gentleman informed them that if the ladies still continued Catholics he would not – nor, indeed, could he lawfully – join them in wedlock. For, although he considered the vow of chastity which they had taken as in itself illegal, yet it was binding while they continued of the Popish persuasion.

This being communicated to the nuns, they replied 'that the vow they had taken, independent of any religious opinions, was unlawful, as it had been extorted from them by force. They had communicated their sentiments to their confessor soon after being sent to the convent: and he informed them that if they left the convent they would certainly be put to death by their families.'

The young women further informed the officers 'that when their confessor acquainted the Abbess with what had been told him of their strong aversion to a recluse life, she ordered them to be confined in a dungeon and to be fed only on bread and water. They were also severely whipped every day, which at length compelled them to submit.

'This cruel usage and the unnatural restraint in which they lived – the Almighty having evidently created us all to be happy so long as we can be so with innocence – had gradually and long before their acquaintance with the English gentlemen

– infused into their minds doubts of the truth of that religious system which imposed and countenanced such hardships: or could suppose a Being, like God, could approve of them.

'In short, they were ready to embrace the Protestant faith if the worthy Chaplain would have the goodness to undertake the task of instructing them.'

During the whole of these transactions, which were communicated to General Blakeney, he gave strict and particular orders that no force or compulsion should, on any account, or under any pretence, be made use of.

Catholic clergymen, and the friends of the ladies, were also permitted to visit, and exhort, and to persuade. But liberty of person and opinion was not to be violated; the general observing on the occasion that he was heartily sorry for what had happened; and – if he could – would have prevented it. But, from the turn things had taken, and the island being for the present under the dominion of the King of England, the principles of a free government must not be departed from.

The affair greatly interested the public mind, and considerably agitated the clergy, regular as well as secular.

One peculiarity was observed: the doors and windows of the room where the nuns slept were sealed every night in the presence of their friends and the confessor, and opened before them in the morning, to satisfy the parents of the young women that no illicit intercourse was carried on.

At length, in spite of public clamour and private remonstrance, the fair Minorquines renounced the faith and errors of the church of Rome; and, having declared themselves Protestants, the same day received and conferred happiness by being married to their military lovers. Their associate in this escape, imitating their avowal of the Protestant persuasion, not long after became the wife of an English gentleman.

So there you are; angels to some are devils to others; and the British, with their worldwide interests for so long, have had their share of both roles.

One of the great points of difference, and intersection, between the British and foreigners for centuries has been religion: whether

in war, missionary work or − more recently − British converts
to Islam.

There was not much of that kind of nonsense at the time of
such as Charles M. Doughty, the Arabian explorer, who positively
gloried in going among the Arabs and calling himself a Christian,
travelling under the name of Khalil. He recalls an incident while
he was watching pilgrims setting out for Mecca[2]:

> One who walked by in the company of some Baghdad
> merchants, clad like them and girded in a *kambaz*, stayed
> to speak with me.
> I asked, 'What did he seek?'
> I thought the Haji would say medicines, but he answered,
> 'If I speak in the French language, will you understand me?'
> I beheld a pale alien's face with a chestnut beard: who has
> not met with the like in the mixed cities of the Levant?
> He responded, 'I am an Italian, a Piedmontese of Turin.'
> 'And what brings you hither, upon this hazardous voyage?
> Good Lord! You might have your throat cut among them;
> are you a Moslem?'
> 'Ay.'
> 'You confess their 'None ilah [God] but Ullah, and
> Mahound, apostle of Ullah', which they shall never hear me
> utter, may Ullah confound them?'
> 'Ay, I say it, and I am a Moslem; as such I make this
> pilgrimage.'

Doughty obviously couldn't do much with the man, foreigner
or not, though he did give him a piece of his mind. The explorer
himself had trouble enough dealing with the Arabs. He rambled
on to them about his religious beliefs and how they would not
shift him from them − never seeming to realise that there were
Christians among the Arabs before there were Muslims, there
are still millions of them and that the Koran itself enjoins the
faithful to be kind to them, as the nearest in belief to Islam.

The Arabs, on their part, were convinced that he was looking
for buried treasure, and wanted a share. Here we find Doughty
dealing with these sometimes tiresome foreigners, who believed
that treasures are guarded by *Jan*, genies:

> I passed for a seeker of treasures with some who had seen

me sitting under the great acacia, which they believe to be possessed by the Jan at El-Hajr. Now they said to me:

'Did'st thou take up anything, Khalil, tell us boldly?'

And a neighbour whispered in my ear, 'Tell thy counsel to me only, good Khalil, and I will keep it close.'

'There is no lore,' I answered, 'to find treasures. Your finders are I know not what ignorant sots, and so are all that believe in their imposture.'

'God wot it may be so, Khalil is an honest-speaking man; but in roaming up and down, you lighted upon naught? Hearken! We grant you are disinterested – have patience! And say only, if you find a thing will you not give some of it to your Uncle Zeyd?'

'The whole, I promise you.'

'*Wallah*, in Khalil's talk is sincerity, but what does he, always asking of the Arabs a hundred vain questions? Though thou shouldst know, O Khalil, the name of all our camping grounds and of every jebel [hill] what were all this worth when thou wert at home, in a far country? If thou be'st no spy, how can the Arabs think thee a man of good understanding?' ...

Many times good beduin friends predicted to me this sharp ending of my incurable imprudence, when leaving their friendly tribes I should pass through strange vales: but as I lingered long in the country, I afterwards came almost no-whither, where some fair report was not already wafted before me.

'Friends,' I have said, 'I am come to you in no disguises; I have hidden nothing from you; I have always acknowledged myself a Nasrany [Christian], which was a name infamous among you.'

Doughty was so fond of Arabia that his books are written in a form of English which he himself contrived: a sort of alternative-biblical, as though translated somewhat literally from the Arabic. Living among Arabs, he found them full of curiosity. They were surprised that he was collecting information which seemed to them to be of no use in a far country.

All this despite the equally dogmatic assertion of another expert, William Perry Fogg[3]:

'It is a national trait of the Arabs and the Turks, never to show any surprise or curiosity.'

Of course, the British person cannot always have a one-to-one interchange with foreigners: sometimes the position is far more complicated. I recall being in contact with a delegation of what London likes to call high-flyers, trying for an engineering and commercial contract worth several hundred million dollars in a Middle Eastern capital.

A group of these British captains of industry mustered each morning in their hotel restaurant for breakfast and conversation. My interest was, I suppose, mostly curiosity: I was neither an Arab nor a Turk. I was invited to the conferences as I was supposed to have some clout locally.

One day, when negotiations were not going as well as they might, we were joined at our table by two youngish ladies. They explained that they worked for an NGO (non-governmental organisation) at an aid project nearby. They were being harassed by members of a group from another industrialised country, which was competing for 'our' contract. The leader of the British party reluctantly let them join us.

The following day, two young sprouts of the chinless variety, bouncing like puppies, appeared from the British Embassy, which was giving 'all support' to our gallant delegation. Their news was grim. The British were being smeared with malicious gossip by the rival delegation for taking in the girls. And to make things worse, a revised engineering quotation, vital for renewing negotiations, was unavailable.

'London's computers are down — on the blink!' one cried — the other adding the rather unBritish '*Kaput!*' for emphasis.

'I don't care so much about our reputation, though I'd rather not have had this involvement with the women,' snarled the boss (who liked to be called CDM, *Chef de Mission*) 'but who is to do the new calculations in this godforsaken hole?'

One of the youths said, 'Elizabeth — I mean one of the NGO ladies — is a mathematical genius. She could do it all in her head.'

And so it proved; though, alas, the British side did not get the contract after all. But what really startled me was how history might be seen almost to repeat itself, albeit in a garbled form.

I heard later that the two youths married the two girls. So it all put me in mind of the sudden appearance of the nuns; of their swains, who married them; of the General, playing a part like that of the CDM.

And me? Well, stretching things a bit, I suppose I might just be Khalil/Doughty in the other extract, traveller and writer. I say this only because I was thought, even if only metaphorically, to be a treasure-seeker. When I resumed my sojourn among the British tribes, one of them said to me, 'I hear you didn't find any treasure while you were advising that gang who were after that big contract.' Like Doughty's 'Uncle Zeyd', he continued, uncannily, 'If you have other prospects, you can rely on my discretion. You would share with me, wouldn't you?'

Subtlety, though, is often to be found among the British abroad. They may be uncomfortable with the locals, but with longer-standing rivals they can be in their element.

The ruler of a certain Eastern country was proposing to send his son to England or America to study English. It has for long been thought axiomatic among British officials that overseas students studying in Britain one day will give contracts to benefit British firms and adopt a British outlook and thus should always be encouraged.

Such thinking, still rife in Whitehall, no doubt helps explain why Colonel Gaddafi, General Amin, Pandit Nehru and others have passed time in England.

In the case under review, an American senator was visiting the Ruler, and in the small British community it was feared that he would influence the monarch to send his heir to the United States.

All the greater, therefore, was their consternation to learn that their own local expatriate vicar had agreed to write the speech which the U.S. Senator proposed to give upon being received by the potentate. They were less confused (on those grounds, at least) when the visitor stood before the Head of State and intoned, among others, the following words:

'The American eagle, whether steaming in the waters of the Pacific or rolling through the deserts of North Africa, will not draw in its horns or retreat into its shell, but will play its part on the world stage like the rock of Gibraltar it is.'

Not only did this baffle the royal interpreter, but it guaranteed, to the delight of those of formerly little faith, the heir to the throne's despatch to England.

11

Not A Person, But . . .

'The Saxons weren't clever like the Romans.
They couldn't teach anybody anything except
fighting, and the Britons knew how to do that
themselves pretty much already. They didn't
want the British always hanging round, and
they just killed them or chased them away and
took the land for themselves. So, when the
Saxons had finished their conquering the people
weren't Britons any longer but English.'

— *Kings and Things*[1]

We are constantly told in film and documentary, in song and
story, how refugees and immigrants have been taken in,
encouraged and absorbed. At the time of writing, it is just
announced that five per cent of the population is of Asian,
African and other 'ethnic' (usually, though of course incorrectly,
taken to mean non-Caucasian) origins. Although these newcomers
may not always be treated well, their predecessors — Hugenots,
French aristocrats and Jews — have become part of traditional
folklore. Their stories are touching; for instance, the gentle, even
saintly, Protestant weavers, driven from their homes by
Continental religious fanaticism, in due course paying back their
hosts by setting up flourishing industries.

How much more peculiar then to observe that the highest in
the land — the Royal Family, no less — are constantly castigated
in the newspapers for being Germans. Indeed, as late as 1972
the Queen was jeered at by Stirling University students shouting
'Go home, you Hun'.[2] What is the Group Mind up to now? Is
it that the English, all being foreigners in the first place, try to
see everyone else in a similar light?

I have a German friend who recently averred that the English, particularly the Royal Family, are maintaining an ancient tradition in being German and even Hunnish by repute. After all, he points out:

'Bede, though no Englishman (in the sense of not being Saxon) is known as the Father of English Literature. The Germanic tradition dating from his time (AD 673-735) is the very oldest traceable one in the country's literature. I am sure that many people in Britain must be proud of their Germanic roots.'

I plead guilty to not being Saxon, Hunnish, Germanic or even Celtic: but I wouldn't bet on it.

Indeed, in some country places, people from elsewhere, English all, are known as 'foreign'. The manufacture of foreigners is a beguiling thought: the various social classes in Britain could be thought of as foreigners one to another: for what is a foreigner if not someone who speaks and dresses differently, eats and drinks differently, acts differently?

The English were among the various groups of foreigners who were settled — or settling — in England after the Romans left, and used to be called Germans and even Huns by the natives, says the Venerable Bede. But surely this is too rigid, too Continental an explanation for the English character?

If we return to our investigation, I think that we shall eventually show something more compelling, more interesting, than that.

As I have noted, it has long been quite acceptable, romantic even, for an Englishman to have a gipsy grandmother (and thus Indian ancestry). The renowned English explorer of Arabia, Abdullah St. John Philby (father of the spy, Kim Philby) boasted of being born a gipsy: though his son is generally represented as being of patrician stock. This sort of thing is a typical British eccentricity.

One is constantly reminded by media and literature alike that Winston Churchill was part-Cherokee; that the best British generals were Irish, the greatest engineers Scots, and the cleverest politicians Welsh, in whole or part.

English people love to describe themselves as 'mongrels'. But British Fascists, advocating racial purity, have roamed the streets of London; Bengali and other immigrants are regularly beaten up in the East End; newspapers attacking the Frogs, Krauts, Ice-creamer Italians and wogs of all kinds sell copies by the million daily.

A German-inspired school, Gordonstoun, is established in Britain: in due course to make a proper Englishman out of, among others, the Prince of Wales.

Whatever can it all mean?

'When the British support anyone, they do so through thick and thin,' says a foreigner, besotted with this country like some of the rest of us, and quoted in a newspaper yesterday.

I am glad to hear it: for in today's issue of a government-supporting broadsheet I read that 'the Government's policy smacks of cowardice and lunacy.' That is support? Then what would opposition be – killing the Party by fast publicity instead of slow? And a writer in an otherwise highly patriotic paper calls the heir to the Throne the 'Clown Prince'. That, I believe, may even be against the law.

This sort of thing is happening all the time. The Royal Correspondent of the *Daily Mail* reveals (exclusively) that the golden orb which surmounted the Prince's purpose-made crown on his investiture in Wales 'conceals a bizarre secret'. It was, in fact, a gilded ping-pong ball. Buckingham Palace expressed thanks for the information.

Not to mention the discovery – also for some reason published in the daily Press – made by Mr. John Keelan, a retired auditor from Chelmsford. He 'has been on the trail five years' and has found he has 'an arsonist as an ancestor in common with the Queen.'

Yet, in spite of all this, is it not the Group Mind which brings out masses of people to vote for that very administration which is suspected of cowardice and lunacy? Does the Group Mind not concur in the appointment of the Heir to the Throne; even moving people to turn out in their dozens, hundreds, thousands, to see and welcome him wherever he goes?

So, what do you think is really going on?

At least, you might think, the British like their own country well enough to stay here, in spite of the weather. Oh, really? Did you know that six million people – one person in ten – of the UK population already resides abroad? Everything seems to drive them away. Indeed, if the reasons they give for quitting are anything to go by, they seem hardly able to stand anything about their own country.

The reasons? Writers, actors and media people are the most voluble on the subject. Complaints range from Graham Greene's dislike of certain sounds (as already noted, he left Britain because he was 'unable to stand the sound of braying English middle-class voices') to Dr. Jonathan Miller, whose outburst centred around 'rancid and depressing' British spite, stinginess and bourgeois vulgarity, (not to mention 'curious mean-minded minginess'). The latter is headlined:

'I'M FED UP WITH THIS MEAN AND PEEVISH LITTLE LAND.'

He also makes it clear that he 'adores Britain', which, he emphasises, is his country.

Or take Somerset Maugham, in his *The Summing Up*[3]. He seems to prefer shaking the dust of the whole thing indiscriminately off his feet:

'I have never felt entirely myself till I had put at least the Channel between my native country and me.'

Unspecific though he was, we may glean some insight from Maugham's conclusions. He suggests, in the same book, that the English have a 'native lack of precision', which he feels may show an affinity with Eastern thinkers such as Hebrew prophets.

Dr. Miller has worked in Israel, and may well prefer it, implying that one gets more recognition of talent there. Be that as it may, the foregoing is a further hint as to the nature of our ultimate conclusion about the origins of the English attitudes.

The Daily Telegraph, I was glad to note, did not allow the good doctor (as he hates being called) to escape entirely unscathed. After reading many deadpan reports of Miller's opinions, I was becoming reconciled to the chattering classes' approval of almost anything he said, when I found a *Telegraph* leader gently putting the boot in:

'Nothing so enrages the British people as the spectacle of their own kind expressing a preference for foreigners, and especially for foreign pay slips.'

I'm more than glad that that was said. Those of us who reside in the UK would feel rather foolish if no support for it were forthcoming from its own Press. But the evidence is, I am afraid, quite against that viewpoint.

For instance, the BBC's Radio Solent, running a hoax programme on April 1, 1992, claimed that the otherwise 100% English Isle of Wight might really belong to France, because of an ancient link. Its switchboard was flooded by calls, mostly from local people, according to *The Times*, who were wholly in favour of becoming − French.

According to *The Independent Magazine*, figures showed in October 1992 that almost half the people in Britain between the ages of 16 and 24 − 46% of them, to be precise − would like to leave the country for good.

A book on opinion polls published by Thames and Hudson claims that, of all the British, 36% are restless, 14% are lonely, and 21% are bored. This means that no less than 71% are dissatisfied with their lives here.

In a *Sunday Times* article[4], Godfrey Smith says 'we are unquestionably the grubbiest country outside the Third World, and there is plenty of evidence that we have long been so.'

Can this have some connection with the getting-out-of-Britain urge?

I ask this because, on the same page of this important journal of record, Tim McGirk quotes Claire Hardwick, spokesperson for the Keep Britain Tidy Group. She says that it is 'not simply a problem to be solved by clearing up'. She cites sociological studies showing that littering − and far worse crimes − are a symptom of dissatisfaction with our surroundings.

The Daily Telegraph was able to report a German analysis of why the British are discontented:

> 'The desire of Britons to emigrate is in keeping with a centuries-old need to escape the British weather and food.'[5]

The *Suddeutsche Zeitung* was responding to a Gallup poll, which showed that half the population wanted to leave. It noted that 'already in the 16th century, before there was any talk of capitalism, Drake and his gang founded colonies so that they would never have to live in England again ... The Gallup poll merely confirms that the British need an empire again.'

What do they do about it?

Some, whether grumblers or not, really do vote with their feet, though they do it in a characteristically baffling English manner. According to the US Embassy in London, only 5000 British people are admitted to God's Own Country with immigrant visas each year. Five thousand Britons entering America seems clear enough.

But we are dealing with the English: nothing is what it seems. Though five thousand leave these shores, twenty-eight thousand (British Department of Trade statistics) *arrive* as British immigrants annually in the USA. That, at any rate, is what the *Sunday Times Magazine* tells us.

What exactly happens, then? Do they appear in mid-Atlantic? Leave the UK as British but arrive in the USA as Hondurans, Bolivians or Colombians, armed with the alternative passports advertised for sale in The *Herald Tribune* (European Edition) or *The Economist*, just in time to be counted by the US immigration people?

Do they de-materialise at Immigration? And then re-materialise, once inside the USA, for some DoT (UK) official to count them, in due course?

If so, why? By this I mean, both why do all this and why and how do the British authorities manage to count them once in the USA?

And there is yet another mystery. When Paul Vallely, of *The Daily Telegraph*, asked the US Embassy what kind of Brits they wanted, this is the response:

> 'Top notch people ... You know: Nobel scientists, senior bankers, Hollywood actors, professional athletes ... that sort of thing.'[6]

As I can't work out what is going on, I'll dodge the question by saying that the time has surely now come to pull these snippets of evidence together, to see what it is that could account for the strangeness of life among the Brits. Especially the fact that they seem as much *for* something as *against* it, as sincere and energetic in their espousal of a cause as they are to attack and deny it. If you can't guess, then the odds are in favour of your having attended less closely than you might have done to previous writings in this series.

You will recall that it was established in *Darkest England* and *The Natives are Restless*, that the people of England, particularly the Angles, are the newest immigrants into Europe. The Romans and the Greeks, whose culture they (quite possibly fallaciously) claim as their heritage, were Europeans when the Angles were still nomads, and quasi-Oriental ones at that.

Nomads and Easterners. What does this, in turn, mean? In the first place – as we know from studies of communities like Bedouins, Gypsies and Old Testament tribes – such populations do not abide by the manners and concepts of settled peoples. (Even the term 'civilised' is literally derived from the Latin for 'town-dweller'.)

They remain free: free, like the English, to have no written constitution, for example. Why? Because, by its very nature, nomadic life requires people to change in accordance with shifting circumstances. They hate officialdom and rules, and rely heavily on group democracy. All English people know this. They know little or nothing of the history of it – the whats – and are therefore so implausible when they try to explain the whys of their behaviour. And they become increasingly uncomfortable when squeezed by the officialdom and bureaucracy of the EC in Brussels. They 'feel it is wrong' to be as quickly and completely European as they are expected to be. In their turn, the more-established Europeans are baffled by them.

John Mortimer is very perceptive about the British quasi-aversion to towns and cities:

> 'We aren't very good at towns. We have never produced a city to equal Paris or Prague or Vienna. We lack the gregariousness of true city dwellers.'[7]

Nomads are not really gregarious. They have to spend too much time together. They prefer isolation or travelling when they can manage it. Real town-dwellers are gregarious because their situation is the very reverse: their walls keep them apart. They are willing to talk and socialise. They can withdraw behind their walls when they want to.

And there is more. The nomadic mind mimics Nature's flexibility – not the rigid institutions of European-style humanitarian idealism.

What, for example, could be more flexible than the many British Christians I noted in *Darkest England* who believed in Heaven but not in Hell? Incidentally, a lot of these believers actually claimed that Buddhism was a better religion than their own. And there is a continual process of change – almost of debunking. Out of a population of 60 million, for example, the UK has only 2 million committed members of the official Church of England – far fewer than the country's non-Christians. In a generation or two, it is estimated, Muslims will outnumber observant members of the established Church: a new mosque opens every two weeks.

The late Sir Nicholas Fairbairn, MP showed characteristic British irreverence:

'If it was not for the fact that it christens you, marries you and buries you, there would be no place for the Church at all, except for community hymn singing.'[8]

On the other hand, Satanists, with admittedly only about 16,000 communicants, have gained 1000 members in two years.

Perhaps in religion as in more mundane matters – to which I revert with relief – there is a balancing factor at work. Such as the news that 'Trains 10 minutes late will be reclassified as "punctual" to improve the records'.

There has developed among nomads, and with the British, a constructive/destructive tension. It mirrors Nature: something which, though it gives you birth and enables you to grow and flourish, is also trying to kill you at the same time. Plagues, bacteria, wild beasts all belong to Nature; as well as sunsets, flowers and babbling brooks. As with Nature, so with the dichotomy of the English.

Somewhere deep inside, some at least of the English know this. I will never forget the moment when I heard an infuriated Englishman bellowing 'I am not a person: I am a natural force!'

It can be blindingly obvious to anyone who has not been conditioned to think of the English (and their students, the rest of the British) as settled, ancient, a mature urbanised civilisation and so on. Just look, anthropologically and historically, at nomadic tribes and their behaviour.

Indeed, so close is the resemblance to Eastern tribes in a myriad ways that some English people have believed that theirs is a chosen people akin to the Jews. Others have found a startling affinity with the Arab Bedouins or the Pashtuns of the old North-West Frontier.

If you, as an English person, wish to use these explanations to enable foreigners to come to terms with your strangeness — be my guest.

On the other hand, look now at these words by Michael Ignatieff:

> 'The Royal Family is now being torn apart by a uniquely British combination of raging envy and fawning indifference.'[9]

If you find this uncomfortable, do not despair. I have just explained to you that what are taken for negative and subjective characteristics can be seen as something much deeper, much more permanent and far more explicable — and forgivable — than Perfidious Albion. Or even The Dirty Man of Europe, fighting to the last Frenchman and the rest.

Indeed, the time may well come when we find that this Eastern-Nomad-Nature ethos has a greater survival value than all the deeply-treasured but as yet unproven European theories about democracy and State organisation.

One thing it does seem to do is to endow life in Britain with a uniqueness, which can only be tasted *in situ* and then reviewed in the calm of somewhere else. Most people think that you should only do the former: but what about operator-attitude affecting the experiment? And, as foreigners, we should at least do the Brits the courtesy of adopting their amazing discovery of The Study of Culture at a Distance.

12

Culture At A Distance

'Mr. Brian Osborn, a church organist in
Worthing, West Sussex, has had to get the
Japanese word-processor used for printing
hymn sheets reprogrammed after the 'spell-
check' device altered Jesus to Jessica.
　　　　　　 – *The Times*, 3 February 1990

At Lord Bernstein's luncheon table, I was once rude enough to
ask this great English media entrepreneur why his huge Granada
Group did not show more cultural films, documentaries and the
like, on commercial television.

He looked at me like a British workman who'd been asked to
work his day off, and said: 'If we were to give people what they
wanted, we would be transmitting cowboy films, sport and
violence twenty-four hours a day. Is that what you want?'

So, as he was indirectly emphasising, it is easy to criticise when
you don't know all the facts. I notice today, more than a decade
later, commercial TV does not list a single documentary among
the top 30 programmes of the week, according to the Broadcast
Audience Research Board (BARB). Fictional programmes, such
as police series, however, number their viewers in the tens of
millions. Even criminals inform journalists that they learn a lot
from crime programmes.

Until recently, British political parties used to offer all kinds
of interesting inducements to electors if they would only vote for
them. When they got into power, they would say, 'Ah, yes. We
can't do this and that: in fact we have to do the opposite. Taxes
will go up, and so forth. You see, we didn't know all the facts
when in opposition.'

I say until recently, because nowadays so much gets into the

93

newspapers, on the radio and television – and into books – that it is becoming more and more difficult to play that one.

It is still a secretive society in Britain – the most secretive in Europe – but plenty of things about the life here do get into print or are otherwise circulated. So we can carry on our study of Culture at a Distance largely from public sources, with a little admixture of personal experience here and there.

First of all, facts are interesting to the British because they generally go by feeling and not substance. This may explain why books with titles like *Not a Lot of People Know That* and *The Book of Facts* sell uncommonly well. Unexpected facts make people *feel* something. Whether facts are any use to them is not a British concern, in general.

So, dealing in real events as well as feelings should be of help both to the Brits and also to the foreigner (God help him!) trying to understand them.

Let's start with humour: a British hallmark. Most of their own lists of the pre-eminent features of the breed include it, together with a sense of fair play.

A.P. Herbert (Sir Alan Herbert, generally known as A.P.H.) was for long one of the nation's most-liked humorists. In July 1950, he gave the Presidential Address before *The English Association*. We must therefore assume that he knew what he was talking about, and that what he said was authoritative.

'Tell an Englishman that he has no sense of humour,' he says, 'and he will knock you down'. After further remarks in this vein, he continued to tell a story. It seems, some decades later, to be rather laboured and told at inordinate length, so I shall have the temerity to summarise the Master's words.

> A would-be lavatory attendant, poor and illiterate, placed a bet of sixpence on a horse in a race. The horse won, and the man used the winnings to buy, successively, a horse and cart for selling vegetables, and then went into other businesses, trading so well that he finished up as the head of a great multiple store.
>
> He now went to a bank, and asked the manager to accept some of his money as a deposit. When asked to sign his name, he confessed that he could not write.
>
> The manager said: 'Do you realise what a wonderful man

you are? Here you are, a self-made man. You have built up
this business from nothing; and yet you cannot read and write!
Have you ever thought, Mr. Smith, what you might have been
if you had been able to read and write?'

'Yes,' said Mr. Smith. 'I should be a lavatory attendant.'

The moral, according to A.P.H., contains a great philosophy
of life, namely 'never give up hope'.

I tried out the story on various people in London. My cleaning
lady, Mrs. Coggins, said, 'I does the pools. If I wins, I'll never
have to work again. That's better than startin' wif a horse an'
cart.'

Her husband, Mr. Albert Coggins, said: 'You gets into the
income-tax net that way, startin' businesses and the like. Leave
it out, I say.'

The man who came to clear the gutters said, 'Get away with
you. It just ain't true. Thass like the kind of stuff wot they try
to tell you in church, innit?'

I did get one further reaction, though. While quizzing Mrs.
Coggins, I had left the radio on. There came a news bulletin,
about a mine disaster in the Far East. It killed 500 Chinese, 200
Koreans, up to 100 Russians, and one Englishman, an engineer.

'Pore feller,' said Mrs. Coggins. 'Wot a disaster for 'im.
Wonder if 'e suffered?'

But I am dealing with humour, with special reference, of
course, to foreigners: so I shall return to it now.

I suppose the exception proves the rule, but I was rather
discountenanced to read that the British establishment had taken
a German Karneval (equivalent to April Fool) joke seriously.

'I thought you British,' said a German official, 'were supposed
to have a sense of humour.'

British government officials at the very highest level had been
complaining about Teutonic arrogance to the German Embassy
in London. Surely the joke must have been very subtle or very
offensive?

A special protocol, went the hoax story, was to be added to
the conclusions of the Maastricht summit:

Although the protocol recognised the Scottish origins of the
bagpipe, under pressure from the German side it had been
accepted that the Dudelsheim influence was 'unmistakable'

and the characteristic pipes originated from Hesse, a land of great piping culture. The bagpipes were therefore to be known as the Dudelsack.[1]

I wonder why the British were interesting themselves in the matter? Surely they could have consulted a British source — say Haydn's *Dictionary of Dates*[2], where we find, clearly and concisely, on page 67, that the bagpipes are originally not very British:

> 'BAGPIPE, an ancient Greek and Roman instrument. On a piece of ancient Grecian sculpture, now in Rome, a bagpiper is represented dressed like a modern highlander. Nero is said to have played upon a bagpipe.'

The *Oxford English Dictionary*, it is true, says the bagpipes are:

> 'Formerly a favourite English rural musical instrument, now chiefly used in the Scottish Highlands and in Ireland.'

But the OED's first citation of the pipes' use is Chaucer: over 1300 years later than Nero's time: and the Greeks and Romans may well have been using them for aeons before that.

I next turned to Philip Ward's excellent *A Dictionary of Common Fallacies*[3] to see whether British authorities were historically correct in reproving the Germans. Again, it seems as if the Greeks and Italians, rather than anyone else, should have been in there pitching: they undoubtedly have primacy:

> 'THE BAGPIPE ... An instrument of great antiquity, known to the ancient Greeks as the *askaulos* or *symphoneia,* and to the Romans as *tibia utricularis*. It is the French *cornemuse*, the Italian *cornamosa*, and the German *sackpfeife*. The bagpipe appears on a coin of Nero's time and Nero himself is reputed (by Suetonius and Dion Chrysostomos) to have played it. Chaucer's miller performed on it: "A bagpipe well couth he blowe and sowne" [c 1386]. The Highland bagpipe is just one of a hundred variants.'[4]

I have myself seen the bagpipes used among the rural Greeks of today. They are well known in the Afghan mountains, a land which had, for centuries after its conquest by Alexander, a Greek culture. I have also seen bagpipes in Spain, anciently known there as *Gahita* or al-Agata (from which the expression 'see you later, alligator' is said to derive – dating from the period when they were used in Moorish-influenced West Africa).

Another Arabic word for 'bagpipe', spread under the ancient Saracenic empires from the borders of China to the Balkans, is *Mizmar al-Qirbat*. This means, quite unequivocally I should have thought, 'Pipe of the goatskin bag'.

Why should the British get involved at all? That is the question which the foreigner might well ask. Their own reference books supply all the facts they need to let them out of the controversy altogether. Perhaps the bagpipe is known and used in so many cultures that the Brits became possessive about them while studying Culture at a Distance.

Indeed in days gone by, they might have answered the Germans' attack by pointing out that bagpipes were used in Greece centuries before the Hessian Dudelsheim, near Frankfurt.

For some reason, the whole strange matter revolved in my mind, awaiting some resolution. Nearly a year passed before a more plausible explanation, almost an Occam's Razor of a thing, suddenly appeared on my study table. It came in the obituary of Sir Andrew Gilchrist, 'one of the most colourful British diplomats of his time'.[5]

Sir Andrew (to cut a long story short) was Ambassador to Indonesia in 1963, at the time of the 'confrontation' caused by the establishment of the federation of Malaysia. A crowd of 5000 attacked the British Embassy in Jakarta, and began smashing the windows with stones. In the face of this disturbance, Major Muir Walker, the assistant military attaché who was formerly of the SAS, appeared draped in bagpipes and proceeded to walk up and down slowly in front of the building, playing suitable melodies on the fearsome Scots instrument. The mob, astonished, stopped the attack and dispersed.

I rather think that the Foreign Office's interest in, even reverence for, the pipes may date from these events. Sir Andrew and his compatriot, it is true, survived. But the newspaper account leaves it unsaid whether we are expected to gather that the bagpipes averted or exacerbated calamity, for:

'This was "Stone Monday". Two days later – on "Ash Wednesday" – the mob reappeared and burned the embassy to the ground. Gilchrist was lucky to escape with his life.'

The bagpipes are obviously something of greater moment than many of us have suspected ...

Of course, people in Britain are in some ways more serious than they were. It is no longer thought automatically funny to laugh at foreigners. Prince Philip's reference to 'slitty-eyed' Far Easterners, which went down like a lead balloon, was proof enough of that. Yet the funny, very foreign, eponymous figure in my trilogy of *Mulla Nasrudin* books, has been selling well for decades in English, as well as in other languages.

On its own, I don't think that the study of culture at a distance really pays off. Sidney Bernstein thought that too much of the Wild West was unsuitable for the British television mass-audience. It might even be (and often is) questioned whether the kind of thing which is currently transmitted as cultural material is any better. And the noble Lord, who once travelled extensively in Spain, tried to stop people from using the word 'Granada', which he claimed for his TV enterprises. Even the study of culture at close quarters – in this case Andalucia – did not tell him that you can't adopt and monopolise the name of a full-blown city.

The Study of Culture at a Distance, of course, was merely named, not really pioneered, by academics. Long before the notion came into existence, I was one of its many victims. Surely nothing else could have produced the stock of knowledge of the man in the Sudan who told me that England was 'full of cruel lords' who constantly pursued foxes and knouted the peasantry?[6] Or the Arab who denounced me as a fraud for saying, contrary to what he had heard, that it was not blazing hot all year round in Manchester. Or the Indian who thought I'd never been to England because I didn't know that 'two bell' meant a semi-soft-boiled egg.

And the process, whatever it is, still goes on. It happens before our eyes every day. If you look up *Black's Medical Dictionary* (34th Edition), these words may well meet your eyes:

'LEGS, inequality of: this may be due to one leg being longer or shorter than the other.'

Or, in the British *Reader's Digest*, quoting – it is true – *The*

Kiplinger Magazine:

> 'Too frequent baths are often the cause of dry, itchy skin ... Nearly everyone may benefit by cutting down on baths and showers.'

Admittedly, this is advice for older people and colder weather, but − as numerous studies show − people tend to skim what they read. This could well be a factor in Culture-at-a-Distance beliefs.

The English firmly believe that they are eccentric: or, rather, that their country is full of the egregious. They can go so far, in unguarded moments, as to believe that they alone are capable of eccentricity.

How do I know? Read this obituary extract:[7]

> 'Where there was Wim Van Leer there was life. Had he been English he might have been described as a typical eccentric. As a Dutchman he was harder to classify.'

So, are the British the eccentrics par excellence?

Really vast numbers of them are undeniably conformist: wearing similar shell-suits or dinner-jackets, filling Wembley Stadium or pouring morning and evening in and out of mass conurbations to work, lining up for Social Security money, and the rest. In some Italian resorts they are even known as The Interchangeables.

Some foreigners get quite depressed by the conformity. Even in 1937 Kurt von Stutterheim could write[8]:

> 'When an Englishman tries to imagine what is most likely to impress the stranger within his gates, he flatters himself that it is his individualism. In fact the foreigner wherever he looks sees standards and clichés and conventions, and is apt to be somewhat disappointed.'

When I started to look into the matter myself, I discovered that, though many foreigners think that the British are mad, it is the British (and especially the English) who tend to keep the image of eccentricity bright. It's even been suggested in the Press that eccentricity is what makes Britain great. Interestingly enough for such an important matter, it was not until recently that the subject was studied in a proper academic framework.

Dr. David Weeks, a principal clinical psychologist at the Royal Edinburgh Hospital, located a hundred 'genuine eccentrics'. These included 'a man who abseils down tower blocks dressed as a pink elephant, a long-distance tricyclist whose home is a bombed-out house in Belfast and a man who made his dog a company director.'

On the books of the research team were:

'A lady in Devon with 7000 gnomes and pixies in her garden, a man called Mangelwurzel who drove in reverse from Sheffield to Huddersfield by night, and a Briton who lived the life of Davy Crockett. In Scotland, the researchers located a cave dweller whose home was partly submerged by every high tide.'

These, I repeat, are all 'identified as helping to make Britain great.'

What makes an eccentric? I had often wondered; and had frequently mis-categorised them. I would have added to their number the Police Crime Prevention Officer who visited my house in the country one day. I said: 'I suppose this board, with every house key on it plainly labelled, should be shifted from its current place, where it is passed by every casual visitor?'

He gave me a long and steady look. 'No,' he said, 'that would be takin' things a bit far, wouldn't it?'

How do I know he wasn't eccentric? Because, according to the Edinburgh discoveries, eccentrics are characterised by their 'insatiable curiosity, unfailing inventiveness and obsessive interests.' None of these was detectable in the case of PC Plod.

Then, again, we hear that 'as many as one in 200 of the population' may be eccentric.

Was not a single one of them listening, then, when Hans Keller broadcast 'senseless noise' instead of music: and nobody spotted it.

Unless, of course, you can call eccentric the critic in *The Times* who remarked that 'some sections in the middle were rather weak'.[9]

Blame it on the influence of academia if you wish, but I feel that there is also a sense in which the research itself is skewed; even eccentric. Can you imagine, for instance, a genuine eccentric answering a newspaper advertisement calling for eccentrics?

But that was the way in which the subjects of the survey were located. Why, for instance, were recommendations from non-eccentrics (surely the ones to judge) excluded? And how was it determined that some of the people were not just plain exhibitionists?

Of course, there may be perfectly good reasons, not disclosed in the report just quoted, to answer our queries. This, indeed, is one of the problems of the Study of Culture at a Distance: it is, after all, At a Distance.

If you were abroad, what would you make of the seventy-two-year-old man, a retired schoolmaster, who was jailed for 70 days? It was his twenty-first prison sentence. His crime was that he refused to wear a crash-helmet when riding his motorcycle. He was campaigning for the right to dispense with a helmet, to be on equal terms with Sikhs in Britain, who had been accorded that privilege.[10]

Whether you knew the reason or not (I don't) you might still be perplexed by Britain's Worm-Charming championship. This takes place in Devon: worms are charmed from the ground by any legitimate means. Then again there is the important information that a nun won a bet of double or quits with a millionaire, by reciting correctly the names of the Wolves team which lost the 1939 FA Cup Final to Portsmouth.[11]

Culture at a Distance study can tell us something about the British monarchs: they were usually flat broke in the past, however much they coined it later. Mrs. Shirley Berry, a former Keeper of the Metalwork Department of the Victoria and Albert Museum in London (and she should know) revealed something unsuspected about the Crown Jewels, shown at the Tower of London:

> 'She has found that, for 250 years,' says Peter Watson of *The Observer* 'many of the jewels on public view were, not to put too fine a point on it, fakes ... Thus the thousands and thousands of people, over the centuries, who paid good money to see the jewels, were duped.'

Study the culture as you may, the facts and half-beliefs persist and the enigmas remain. What is the point of litter bins which talk as at Taunton, Somerset? How could it be that *both* Lord Salisbury and Gladstone said 'We are part of the community of

Europe and we must do our duty as such'? (*Oxford Dictionary of Quotations*). Why did Mr. Major, at the time the British Prime Minister, recommend 'a redundant manager trying to escape Britain's lengthening dole queues' to 'move to France if you need a job'?[12]

One justification for carrying on the Study of Culture from a Distance could well be that there is a better perspective from afar. This thought enables me to offer, for overseas students, a further selection of tales from England.

A British Civil Servant was accused under the Official Secrets Act of passing classified information to a colleague. This was not only already known to the recipient but was about – toy typewriters.

A headless ghost, dressed in Elizabethan costume haunted the Queen's bank – Coutts & Co. – in London for a time. Finally an (unpaid) clairaudient expert was commissioned to help release the presumably 'earthbound spirit'. The ghost was persuaded by this expert, Mr. Eddie Burks, to depart, after a conversation of only 45 minutes.[13]

Each and every anecdote in this book is true, so far as I have been able to check. Even this one:

Britain is the headquarters of the liars of the world – and proud of it. 'Masters of mendacity, inaccuracy and falsehood gathered in a secluded Lake District pub to fight for the title of Biggest Liar in the World.'[14]

I am sure you are dying to know what happened. Well, the reigning champion won with 'a tale about his alleged singing career. "I was known as the Pavarotti of the Pennines," he said, "I was chased by millions."'

There is only one snag: 'Since I won the title, I can't get people to believe a word I say.' As a writer, I can sympathise with that. But, then again, perhaps he was lying.

13

Dealing With Foreigners I:
Disinformation

Humans first set foot in Britain more than half
a million years ago ... However, ancient
Britons appear to have stayed on only when the
weather was bad − a bizarre discovery that
sheds new light on the British character.
− John Wymer,
Norfolk Archaeological Unit[1]

It seems, from the above, that even before the arrival of the
Angles there was something pretty rum about Britain. As John
Wymer, of the Norfolk Archaeological Unit, puts it, speaking
of the discoveries: 'All we can say is that ancient Britons seem
to have had a mysterious urge to hang about in the cold and rain.'

Perhaps, of course, the original Britons didn't like visitors,
foreigners above all; and, like the present-day Brits, they went
abroad during the summer tripper season.

After all, if this were so, they would only be precursors of our
own contemporary, the author A.N. Wilson:

'What England needs is fewer people. More trees. And a
ruinously strong pound to discourage all potential Continental
or transatlantic trippers.'[2]

Of course, the methods used by the British to avoid foreigners
have been considerably finessed since prehistoric times. They no
longer need to flee abroad. Instead, they have developed a
sophisticated strategy for preventing foreigners from ever braving
these shores.

Most English people manage to operate this technique without being consciously aware of it. There are two parts to the procedure. The first is to give yourself a bad Press. The second is to call foreigners every name under the sun. In a word, scare them off.

So important, so fundamental, are these twin planks of British behaviour towards foreigners, that I shall devote the next two chapters to examining them in more detail.

We have heard something of the crucial role played by the Press in spreading reports calculated to dissuade foreigners from visiting these shores. For instance, I'd think twice about coming here upon reading that the country has a higher proportion of its population in jail than any other Western country. I would reason that either more people here are criminals, which is no fun for visitors, or else they are being treated harshly and I might be so treated myself.

But one should always read news stories carefully and, if possible, in conjunction with other available data. Prison in Britain might be just what our visitor is looking for. After all, a report by the National Association for the Care and Resettlement of Offenders notes that one night in a police cell costs more than a room at London's Ritz Hotel. The cost of keeping a burglar in a treatment centre in 1993 according to the *Daily Mail* was nearly £200,000 in a year. To keep a room at the Savoy Hotel, one of London's best, would be £62,000. To keep a boy at one of England's premier schools, Eton College, costs a mere £11,610 a year.

The very existence of international wire services seems designed to distribute stories carefully selected to deter would-be tourists and immigrants:

LEGALISE ALL DRUGS SAYS JUDGE

POLL: QUALITIES MOST ADMIRED BY BRITONS –
POLITENESS CAME LAST

DRINKING WATER CONTAMINATED BY GARDEN
SPRAYS

Even Buckingham Palace's water, and that of Parliament is

involved, says the latter piece. And lest the visitor should fail to take the hint, another newpaper piece tells of a mammoth Festival of British Food and Farming, opened at Hyde Park by Her Majesty one summer. Pigs were there, the best from all over the country, and:

PIGS TURN NOSES UP AT LONDON'S WATER

... these animals were very, very hot, but the water was too tainted even for pigs to fancy ... [they] promptly turned up their noses when they were given London water to drink ...

Muslims should note that pigs, in England, seem to have a specially privileged position. David Edwards, of the Derby Playhouse discovered that 'Hiring a pig costs more than twice the weekly wages of an actor.'

Well, every country has its little ways, you might reason. On the plus side, England has Shakespeare, Wimbledon, the Lake District, the Changing of the Guard. Time for the English to hit back again. There isn't really anything much of interest to see here at all. Honest, Guv:

HOLE ENTERS THE LIST OF HISTORIC SIGHTS. An eight-foot deep water-filled hole on a Somerset farm has been looked into by Government experts and declared a site of national historic interest.[3]

What's more, you can forget shopping: a lot of the shops aren't actually British-owned, and few sell British goods nowadays. If you want Aquascutum, you're buying from the Japanese. Groceries and department-store items? The Egyptians will be glad to help you. As to clothing – German stores are well thought of. Even your newspaper may be owned by an Australian, and the auctioneers where you buy your very British antiques may well be American.

If you are a gourmet, you can always sustain yourself on that good old English fare of Kentucky fried chicken, or a hamburger – or Indian, Chinese, Greek, Turkish and Vietnamese takeaways.

What's more the food sounds a bit expensive. Take this headline:

PRIVATE PATIENTS 'CHARGED £195 A DAY FOR TEA IN PLASTIC CUPS.'

Patients in a London hospital, it transpires, were billed £1,200 a day for food they never received. Although, come to think of it, lots of foreigners don't drink tea, whatever the composition of the cups.

Snacks, like sandwiches, sound a much better bet. Or do they?

The British Sandwich Association has warned: 'Environmental health officers are increasingly alarmed by the standard of sandwiches they test.'

The Group Mind does its job well. And it is by no means finished. Let's nip down to the *bahnhof* paper stall or *petit-kiosk*, get an armful of London papers, and see how things look from the British end:

BRITAIN 'SECOND ONLY TO PORTUGAL IN POVERTY' – (*The Observer*)

CHURCH ACCUSED OF RACISM – (*Sunday Telegraph*)

BRITISH WOMEN: THE LAGGARDS OF EUROPE – (*Royal Society of Arts Journal*)

SOME BRITISH FISH UNSAFE TO EAT, MINISTERS ADMIT (*Independent on Sunday*)

Of course, forewarned is forearmed; you always have to make sacrifices when you travel. To see original landscapes of Turner, the living democracy of the House of Commons, the Beefeaters of the Tower, the waxworks at Madame Tussaud's, we can put up with some inconveniences.

Our intending tourists may be made of too robust material to be put off by a few headlines. After all, they might reason, their foreign currency could even help the beleaguered little island, put some health into the unhealthy, could encourage the female laggards. As for work disasters, we are not going to seek employment there, so the problem should not arise.

The unsafe fish meals? Avoid Fridays if you are a Catholic seems the best advice. Oh, yes: and Christmas. According to a Ambassador of Finland at the Court of St. James's, Christmas puddings and mince pies:

'... are a very British thing and, I suspect, one which the British might not be able to persuade the rest of the world to buy.'[4]

Has he been got at by the Group Mind's auto-disinformation programme? I must confess to liking both the puddings and the pies myself, even though a foreigner. And I, for one, have never met anyone who disliked them, either. And you have the bonus — in some countries you can dine out on the tale — that mince pies contain no meat.

The influence seems to be spreading through the diplomatic world. *The Times* Diary reports the United States Ambassador in London listing 'exactly what he valued about being an American':

'Freedom from Marmite, from roundabouts, from three-prong plugs, from all-day cricket, and from EastEnders.'[5]

Perhaps the new Ambassador had not got his finger on the pulse of Britain as firmly as he might. The market researchers Mintel had determined years before that 'Cricket, the game we gave the world, has been bowled out at home'. Only three per cent of people play it, and 'it is now one of the nation's most unpopular sports'. Trust the old English Group Mind to keep ahead of everyone.

And freedom! At least that is something that everyone expects to find in this pioneer land of human rights, this home of Magna Carta, this cradle of liberty. To prepare ourselves in this regard, we may turn to the United Nations Table of Humanities (1991) to confirm the freedoms and people-participation of this great home of democracy. But someone (probably a British disinformation expert from the Group Mind) has been here first:

'In world ratings by the United Nations, the USA was 13th, and the United Kingdom 16th in democracy on the planet.'

So, if democratically-minded, do not plan to visit Britain.

There is always a hullabaloo about education going on in Britain: those in charge don't seem to like it very much: as the saying, quoted in several reference books, has it, they tend to believe that:

LEARNING MAKES THE WISE WISER, BUT THE FOOL MORE FOOLISH

University professors and other teachers hoping for a welcome here should heed the words of the former Prime Minister, John Major:

> 'The Prime Minister didn't achieve many academic qualifications. And here is his verdict on those gained by his friends ... THEY'RE WHOLLY USELESS!'[6]

So what other vocations might be welcome here? Perhaps a scientist could visit colleagues or obtain some support for his or her ideas?

> 'Scientists are arrogant, incapable of managing their own affairs, and think that they have a divine right to public funds.' (Sir Douglas Hague)[7]

Professional architects?

> 'I wouldn't have a qualified architect in the office. They're just argumentative. They've got lots of political ideas, which aren't of interest to me; they want a partnership, they're quarrelsome, they're lazy, they arrive late. *They don't shave.*' (Quinlan Terry, Architect)[8]

Mind you, you could always define yourself by contraries, as it were. An architect desirous of visiting the country (even after reading the foregoing) could manage an effective disguise by: getting into no arguments, never referring to partnerships, avoiding politics, being energetic, arriving on time, and (if a man, of course) shaving extra closely.

Foreigners may be tempted by the idea of a study trip, to take part in all those college rags and toast crumpets by the roaring Oxbridge study fires. Then again, maybe not:

PROFESSOR PREDICTS BRITISH DEGREES WILL BE WORLD'S WORST[9]

Faced with the mass creation of 28 new universities in June 1992, Michael Dummett, Wykeham Professor of Logic at Oxford, warned 'degrees from British universities will cease to be respected'. There doesn't seem to have been any such effect. But who would try conclusions with an Oxford Professor of Logic?

If the British want foreigners to stay away so strongly, are they ready to give them incentives to remain in their own countries, especially those in the Third World? It doesn't seem like it:

> 'Britain and the United States are the meanest industrial countries when it comes to giving foreign aid – and most of that does not go where it should.'[10]

Do I hear you say that this selection of quotations is unrepresentative, that I'm exaggerating by concentrating them? Not in the least: 700,000 complaints made annually in the United Kingdom are 'just the tip of the iceberg', according to the Office of Fair Trading: they could total 'up to 70 million a year if the British could overcome their feelings that to complain in public is a sign of bad breeding'.

The Disinformation Programme is, it seems, only just getting into its stride. We may now expect an increased torrent of grievances about failed and fraudulent businesses, bank charges, credit cards, car sales, estate agents, slipshod workmanship, holiday firms, faulty electrical goods – to mention but a few of the complaints even now regularly handled by the Office.

Foreigners intending to live in the country, or even to deal with British businesspeople, might note the OFT's warning:

> 'The market may deal with unsatisfactory business practices eventually, but in the meantime – and it can be a very long meantime – real people do suffer real damage. In some cases, a few people suffer acute and serious harm; in others, large numbers of people lose out, but less severely.'

Right: we may make a note to be careful of businesses in case they are fraudulent, of manufactured goods (especially electrical) because they may be faulty, avoid credit cards and banks, hire or buy no cars, take no holidays without careful scrutiny, ('TRAVEL AGENTS ARE INCOMPETENT AND LAZY SAYS *WHICH?*') – and treat estate agents with the greatest caution.

I overheard a Punjabi grocer explaining how Britain works to a student compatriot on a study tour at the corner shop not so long ago. It seems as good a conclusion as any to this part of our review: 'Yes, they call it a democracy here; but it is rather closer to what we, in Pakistan, used to call "Guided Democracy".'

He had been approached by the other man with a list, asking for clarification of the roles of the nine High Officers of the Realm. I took a copy:

The Lord High Steward
The Lord High Chancellor
The Lord High Treasurer
The Lord President of the Council
The Lord Privy Seal
The Lord Great Chamberlain
The Lord High Constable
The Lord High Admiral
The Earl Marshal.

No, I wasn't able to help, either.

So far, I have asked three hundred people, mostly British, including an audience of constitutional lawyers. Nobody knew what it all meant. One Chinese lady, from Hong Kong, claimed she knew what two of them meant, but I haven't confirmed that yet.

However brilliant and cunning this programme of Disinformation may seem, it has an even more exciting counterpart. It is best known as 'Deterrence Through Truth' – a ploy so simple yet brilliant it is scarcely a wonder it was left to the British to invent it.

Witness, for instance, John Lanchester who specifically targets a part of London tourists might otherwise be expected to make a beeline for:

'With its stunned tourists, its braying Sloanes, its tanned, pompadoured, £600-Italian-shoe-wearing, BMW-driving British Eurotrash, Knightsbridge induces the feeling of having parachuted deep into enemy territory. Christmas, during which the whole area becomes something out of Hieronymus Bosch, is much worse. In the midst of this collective delirium stands Harvey Nichols.'[11]

And what could be more truthful – or more off-putting, than

the blunt acknowledgement by a British Telecom official[12]:

> 'Most incoming calls are less important than the work they interrupt . . .'

If it is hard to tell real information from its malevolent counterpart, this may be the intention. Even experienced operators like me are frequently at a loss. Can it be true, for instance, that the law is trying to decide 'whether a bee is a domestic animal or a wild beast'?[13]

And how about this:

> 'More than half the population of Britain believes that the National Westminster Bank, British Airways and ITV are, or may be, public services or utilities.'

Thus some findings submitted to the Cabinet Office[14].

But for rather definite disinformation (or is it information?) designed to keep you away from the Sceptred Isle, you should hear about the joys of . . . dirtiness. It transpires that, at a Swiss ski resort, Germans, Italians and French, as well as natives, were notable for their cleanliness. Minette Marin reported in *The Telegraph*:

> 'At first there was something exhilarating about this forceful cleanness . . . how unlike the competing smells of unwashed clothes and bodies on London Transport'

but soon she discovers that this cleanliness is 'in fact a highly developed form of squeamishness'; and:

> 'You do not see this among the English. Squeamishness has rarely been their response to the chaos of life. By reputation the English, rich and poor, do not wash much and are often shabby . . . It is not unusual to see rich men with fraying shirtcuffs.'[15]

Of course, you only have to travel a short distance on the London Underground to know that washing oneself is not a British priority. But with real artistry the British manage this not by using less soap, but *by using more*. Soap sales increase annually. How is the almost poetic outcome achieved? I, a poor foreigner, can hardly be expected to know all the secrets of the

Island Race, but done it is. My proof is a market research study which revealed the French buy only three and a half bars of soap each year — less than half the British total of eight.[16]

However, let us return to Minette Marin's article, and hear her parting shot:

> 'For once I think the English have got it right and the Europeans have got it wrong. Cleanliness may be next to godliness but it is also close to conventionality. I am, despite our filthy streets and urine-scented stairwells, glad the English do not suffer much from it. The English may be the dirtiest and shabbiest of Europeans, but they are still, I believe, the most unconventional, the most inventive, the funniest and best to live with.'

14

Dealing With Foreigners II:
Scaring Them

'Could it be that there is something in the
English, not in the alcohol, that results in
violent aggression? . . . Perhaps it is time we
asked ourselves what it is in our culture that
makes the English potentially such a bellicose
and anarchic people.'
— Dr. John Rae, Letter to *The Times*[1]

The widespread belief that all English (later all British) people
are completely crazy almost certainly originated with a deliberate
ploy by the Group Mind. It is part of the second great method
of preventing foreigners from visiting the place, or even — God
forbid — from talking to an Englishman. This is, of course,
scaring them off.

It could even be the cultural element Dr. Rae is hinting at in
his letter, above. Thus: the tradition of crowd violence, we are
informed, is ancient and honourable. The people who dislike
British football hooligans are the ones who are upstarts. Even
the generally sober London *Times* has been known to editorialise:

Drunken violence at football is one of the oldest English
notions of both fun and heritage . . . hooliganism is a far older
and more traditional part of the English heritage than stately
homes, opera or even the BBC. There is no point in the
minister for English Heritage complaining . . . about English
football fans behaving like wild animals. What else did he
think he was appointed to preserve?[2]

Although *The Times* seems too polite to mention the behaviour

113

of its tabloid stablemates, it is now generally felt abroad that Britain has gone one better than countries which suffer from one terrorist outfit. It has two: the hooligans and the gentlemen of the Press.

Of course, there are lots of ways to frighten foreigners which are more subtle than overt violence. I have seen an Italian cleric reduced to tears on learning that as many as 34% of Britons did not know what Easter was, and that 39% did not know the significance of Good Friday.

A German I know was infuriated when he read on the label of a bottle of sleeping tablets the words: 'May cause drowsiness.'

Some overseas visitors, especially Anglo-Saxon-types (such as many Americans and former colonials), have much more genteel reactions to the confusion which they feel reigns here. One such (Australian-accented) dame was heard to murmur to her companion as they left a London theatre after seeing *Les Miserables*: 'That was very enjoyable, dear: but which one was Les?'

Then there are simple playground taunts, like the Deterrence through Fear attempt at Worcester Cathedral.

US TOURISTS WALK OUT OVER A SKITTING IMAGE

To the British, he was the very model of a modern American tourist.

The cigar-chewing, camera-wielding, baseball-capped, Hawaiian-shirted statue stood in the hallowed portals of Worcester Cathedral.

But when a coachload of real-life US visitors saw it, they thought they were being made to look like dummies . . . and stormed out.[3]

Perhaps the beauty of this story is not that the Dean of Worcester said 'The Americans cannot have any sense of humour'. For me, it is the fact that the organiser was Dr. Carol Spearman − an American.

Over three million North Americans visit Britain each year: or did, before the Worcester Cathedral furore. The organisers of the Worcester incident might have taken heed of earlier advice in the *Sunday Telegraph* to British people about dealing with foreigners. Like an encoded message it is, quite obviously, intended to be read as its opposite:

> Much of British humour, and dinner-table conversation,
> consists of people teasing one another. But Americans — and
> other nationalities — hate being teased . . . Don't make jokes
> about Americans and race, and if you really want to be on
> the safe side, don't make jokes.[4]

British people on the other hand love jokes, whatever the
dangers. London newspapers are full of such headlines as MAN
JOKED AS FIREMAN SAWED OFF LEG (usually referring
to a leg unfortunately trapped by a motor or other crash). But
there can be a downside to this.

One Briton not on his guard against the perils of joking featured
in the case of the

> JOKE THAT WIPED AWAY A SMILE
>   The Dentist's surgery was the last place the nervous patient
> really wanted to be.
>   He joked feebly: 'The way I feel, I wouldn't care if you
> took the lot out . . .'
>   He was given a general anaesthetic on his next visit and
> woke up to find all 22 of his teeth gone.[5]

As if that wasn't enough, the *Journal of the Medical Defence
Union* records that the dentures he got to replace them did not
even fit and had, in turn, to be replaced.

I have just been watching a television programme which
surveys, without comment, new publications. Completely
deadpan, it mentions that a journal called *Traveller's Europe*
printed a survey discovering that 'its respondents consider London
both the safest and also the most dangerous of European cities'.

I wanted to try this one on my more conventional Swiss and
German friends — but found that some, at least, of my German
friends have not visited these shores since they read of another
incident in the *Daily Telegraph*:

> The genuine Bavarian evening arranged to entertain German
> visitors as the highlight of a town-twinning week went down
> like a lead Zeppelin when the oompah band struck up the
> Dad's Army theme tune and some of the British guests sang
> 'Who do you think you're kidding, Mr. Hitler?'

After the true German supper turned out to be saveloy sausage, cabbage and a piece of brown bread, it all proved too much for some guests from Troisdorf near Bonn.

As the Leeds-based Steinhaus Bierkeller Band shouted 'Jawohl!', a few of the 53 German visitors being entertained by the Langbaurgh Twinning Association in Cleveland decided to leave . . .

Things could have been worse. The band planned to do impersonations of Hitler until it was suggested that this might be in bad taste . . . 'The Germans just sat there with their heads bowed as people started singing about Hitler and shouting "Jawohl!"'[6]

Mr. Peter Sotheran, chairman of the Twinning Association, said some English people at the supper were being hypersensitive. That's all right, then.

And, of course, the Brits in this incident were only acting on the assumption that the Germans eat sauerkraut (the French eat more of it) and obey all orders (including to sit and be insulted).

Is there anything in this latter theory? Five German psychology students actually tried to test whether their compatriots were indeed biddable conformists.

According to *Der Spiegel*, they stuck signs saying 'Men only' and 'Women only' on two adjacent telephone boxes in Trier, Rheinland. They were disappointed to find that, of the sample of 69 people, 75% of the men and all but one of the women used the designated box. The one rebellious woman turned out to be French.[7]

Good old-fashioned insults are one of the mainstays of Deterrence Through Fear. There is nothing like calling foreigners names to frighten them off. Strangely, foreigners themselves never seem to quite master this art. Although the other day I did think that a visiting New Yorker had at last cottoned onto the technique at a London dinner party.

He asked our British host: 'Since Bosnia and Geneva are regularly pronounced "Boznyer" and "Genever", how would the English deal with the words if there actually *were* a Boznyer and Genever?'

Quick as a flash came the answer, though in the deceptively languid tones of the Anglean.

'Very much as you Americans would, I suppose, if there were a Tarm and Barb as well as a "Tom" and "Bob".'

He added, for good measure. 'That reminds me: when "international" is "innernational", how *is* inner-national pronounced?'

Now our host, well into what is locally called the teasing and banter mode (which can send foreigners screaming from the room for a good lie down, if not to pack their bags for home) gave tongue again.

'Have you heard this one, by the way? To the English, hell is a place where the Americans talk, the Germans actually *do* own all the sun-loungers beside the pools, where the food is all that foreign muck, the French do the organising, the Serbs are the army and the Irish are the logicians.'

The American did, in fact, make an excuse and go at that moment. He told me later that he had intended to settle his hotel bill and leave that very day. 'What stopped you?' I asked, in characteristic English fashion. (I have become very detribalised myself and so failed to console him, like normal foreigners do . . .)

'I saw something terrible. As I walked to the hotel, I passed a café with a sign BREAKFAST SERVED ALL DAY. That was the last straw. After that I just couldn't take any more.'

I must say, I know the feeling, though after a fair exposure to that kind of thing it troubles me less and less. For instance, this item from *Shropshire What's On* might have paralysed him for hours:

> The Brasserie is open 11.30 am − 3 pm and 6 pm − 11 pm during which time the full Brasserie menu is available (save for the traditional English Breakfast which is only served at lunchtimes.)

'Even a monkey in England would be ahead of any other kind,' gasped my friend. Funny he should have said that, I thought. But, as I didn't know how much medical insurance he had, I didn't tell him I'd just been reading the following press report:

BRITISH WOOLLY MONKEYS TEACH TRICKS OF
SURVIVAL.
A British-born woolly monkey has died while taking part
in a unique and successful project to teach its Brazilian
counterparts how to survive in the wild . . .'

Scare them, by all means, say I; but there are limits, you know.
However, if you are scaring foreigners – or are a foreigner
scared – remember that fright is undiscriminating, like most
other British weapons. Just as foreigner-baiting is learnt by other
people teasing you as a small child at school, so are scare stories
designed to thump the weakest, wherever they are to be found.
I remind you of a certain revealing English joke:
At death's door in hospital, a Scotsman asked for a last request.
Could he hear the bagpipes? A piper was immediately called –
and the Scot recovered completely. There were, however, eleven
other men in his ward. They all died . . .
Then, again, there is this unappetising fact: in 1991 a letter
appeared in *The Times* from the Director General of the British
Safety Council. It complained about the 'alarming condition of
Britain's beaches, now the most polluted in Europe.'

In 1967 my council published a list of Britain's stinking
beaches, which was followed by a clean-up. Twenty-four years
on, I am horrified by the latest findings, indicating that there
has been no improvement, and, if anything, the situation is
getting worse.[8]

The British Government had promised to clean up the country's
scandalously polluted beaches by the 1980s. Twenty years later
– when visitors were still swimming in raw sewage – even the
'safe' beaches were not what they seemed:

ALARM AS BATHERS GET ILL AT 'SAFE' BEACHES.
Bathers have caught sewage-related illnesses on two of
Britain's cleanest tourist beaches, government research
reveals.[9]

Nor is it apparently safe to drink water in Britain – despite
the renowned English mistrust of foreign water. As if in
confirmation of the pigs in Hyde Park mentioned earlier,

Pesticides in water 'break EC limit'. Almost 7 million people in London and the Home Counties are receiving tapwater containing levels of pesticides above the legal standard set by the EC, Friends of the Earth said yesterday.[10]

No wonder British commuters were encouraged to prepare for the worst:

Goodness knows how rail travellers departing from Waterloo reckon their chances of reaching the other end hale and hearty. I note that they are now greeted on the station concourse with a display by an organisation called The Will Registry. Pessimistic passengers can have their wills 'properly drafted' for a minimum fee of £19.95.[11]

The Group Mind is uncannily efficient and selective in its operation, even though the English often claim that they are lazy, negligent and so on. It always hits in the same sort of way. Hence the apparent uniformity of British hotels:

The fascinating thing is not that most British hotels and bed & breakfasts are so awful, but that they all seem to be awful in the same way.[12]

I was interested to note that someone, at least, in Britain had observed this standardisation of the dreadful. The story continues:

The fact they are horrible in more or less an identical fashion is a help, because as soon as you push open the chipped front door (with the smeary window glass) you know immediately you are in for a bad time.

The Group Mind, operating this time what we have identified as the Deterrence Through Truth System, is well into its stride here. But almost everywhere you look in Britain the Press highlights problems which should deter all but the most reckless from daring to come ashore.

One past audit of British banks' performance showed that they had an error rate in dealing with small businesses of no less than 95%. It was announced to the British Psychological Association that juries were swayed not by the evidence, but by the appearance of the accused. And there were even discoveries which seemed especially designed to scare off foreign social workers from trying to collaborate with their British colleagues:

> SOCIAL SCIENTISTS CAN'T COUNT . . . They are not as numerate as their colleagues . . . This means that they find collaboration on international projects or interdisciplinary work difficult in sociology and political science.[13]

Britain is, of course, one of the great generators of news for the media of the world. All journalists know the saying 'Dog bites man is not news; but Man Bites Dog would be news.' And, presto! Britain obliges. The story is flashed by the wire services across the globe. This version appeared in the *Pakistan Times*:

> MAN BITES DOG – LONDON: a man bit his dog (photo above) so badly that it had to undergo surgery . . . [he was] granted a conditional discharge by a magistrate's court in Bristol, western England, banned for keeping a dog for a year, and ordered to pay £23 veterinary fee.

It also seems clear from the above that English magistrates have discovered that the condition called Biting a Dog is self-limiting, and the sufferer recovers after a year.

Both Deterrence Through Fear, dealt with in this chapter, and Deterrence Through Truth, discussed in the previous one, also target the natives of the country. So why are foreigners forever complaining about how immigration people treat them on arrival?

> If you're planning a holiday or even a day trip abroad, don't rely on a British Visitor's Passport to get you back into the country . . . [In the High Court] Mr. Justice Hutchison, rejecting appeal moves by the man who had been refused permission to return to the UK, ruled that a British visitor's passport was not sufficient to get a holder back into the country if challenged.[14]

By all accounts, Britain is a violent, frightening place. *The Independent* shows that even those concerned with health may not be able to live too-healthy lives in England:

HEALTH STAFF REPORT FEAR OF VIOLENCE.

Nearly 90 per cent of health service workers are worried about violence at work . . .

Even scarier, did you know that one-third of British doctors have never been taught to take blood pressure? Eighty-nine per cent were found not to know the difference between mild, moderate and high pressure. The Press gleefully reported this fact as a contribution to Deterrence Through Fear. They added that patients might be denied life-saving treatments because doctors could not perform tests properly.

Of course, one has to be careful anywhere; there are local hazards, like malaria and yellow fever in some countries. And taking blood pressure sounds rather complicated anyhow. Possibly you can't blame doctors for not being able to do it very well. The *British Medical Journal* rallies to the rescue:

GPs SPREAD DISEASE BY MISUSE OF THERMOMETER

As *The Telegraph* quotes the story: 'One in 20 family doctors does not clean his thermometer between patients, a sure way to spread disease . . . The [BMJ] survey also found that only eight per cent of doctors knew how to use a thermometer.'

Perhaps then, it is scarcely a wonder that stories like the following constantly appear in the papers:

HEALTH OF BRITONS AMONG WORST IN DEVELOPED WORLD[15]

This particular example of the genre discussed:

Britain's poor health record among the nations of the developed world, and its failure to improve it in recent years.

It went on to say that among developed countries only the Portuguese, Irish or Belgian lived shorter lives than the British. Citizens of other countries, including Greece, Spain and Italy, lived longer, presumably by staying at home.

Some people *have* learned to benefit from our National Health Service. Not long ago, I was travelling into London from Heathrow Airport by underground train. A gentleman of what the papers call Foreign Appearance got in and sat beside me. He was garrulous and soon began praising the National Health Service.

'Do you know,' he said, 'for years I've been getting my medicines free of charge? Some of them should be dreadfully expensive.'

'Yes, of course,' I said, 'that's the NHS. When you live here, you pay insurance contributions and if you are entitled to free prescriptions you get medicine "free".'

'But that's just the point,' he told me. 'I *don't* live here!'

'Then you can't get free medicine.'

'Oh yes, I can. Do you know how? My brother-in-law just takes my list to his own doctor here, gets free medicine and posts it by airmail to me in my country. Comes straight to my village.'

'That's illegal. Besides, the doctor is supposed to examine the patient . . .'

'You can soon find a pretty compliant one. They only have one minute per consultation, you know.'

'I still say it's illegal . . .'

'Illegal it may be, but people do it, all the time.'

I said, 'If you don't live here, I suppose you are just visiting . . .'

'Not at all, I am immigrating. In fact I have just immigrated. I can get my own free medicine now.'

I said, 'Wasn't it difficult to immigrate? We keep hearing how they are slamming the door and so on.'

'Slam it they may, but not on British Subjects who are also United Kingdom Citizens.'

He brandished a British passport.

'But,' I ventured, 'you said that you were immigrating. Now you say that you are already a British citizen . . .'

He shook his head impatiently. 'You don't know anything, do you?'

'Evidently not.'

'Very well, I'll tell you. British passports are not stamped when you enter the country. So my brother-in-law just posts me his passport, and I come in as him. He is a British citizen, you see.'

'But do you look sufficiently like your brother-in-law?'

'Oh yes. Beard and turban, dark, same height. The British can't tell us apart. What is more, any number of people can do it. We just keep posting the passport back.'

I was trying to work out my next move, as a good citizen, when the train stopped, my fellow beneficiary of the National Health

Service gave a cheery wave, and was out into the night. Maybe, I thought, if loopholes like that were plugged, there might be enough money left over to teach more British doctors how to take and even to interpret blood pressure.

If all this does not frighten a foreigner enough to keep him (or her) away, there's always the food − typically English or otherwise. Of course, it will be awful. Thus the food writer Fay Maschler:

> The English can't bear you to take food seriously. They're frightened of seeming interested.[16]

Tom Jaine, in *The Sunday Times,* backs up her view:

> 'Renowned for putting up with poor food and sloppy service in restaurants, we are usually happy to accept what's dished out − and, in consequence, get the cooking we deserve.'

Whatever you do, avoid health foods. They're positively dangerous. The *Daily Telegraph* tells us that checks carried out by the government found they 'contain more pesticides' than any other foods ... Although Government experts assure us that pesticides in reasonable quantities do not make food unhealthy.

You will survive only if you know how to appear humble − especially in English restaurants, where customers are expected to be obsequious. *The Times* described the dispiriting sight of:

> a clutch of nicely brought-up Londoners, after a vile dinner, cynically served, backing out of some over-priced restaurant while fluting 'Thank you very, *very* much' to a maître d'hotel raised on fish fingers and a wine waiter longing for a pint of draught Bass, preferably tepid.[17]

You may win through in Britain. But possibly not for the kind of behaviour you might expect to see rewarded. According to Craig Brown in the *Mail on Sunday:*

> In Britain, you can eat a hamster, impregnate your secretary, edit a pornographic newspaper or sack a workforce. And, sooner or later, you will be honoured for your efforts.[18]

Remember, though, that you must *not* be any kind of an intellectual:

> But let it be known that you have written a poem or composed a symphony, and you will be shunned by polite society.

Since a very large number of foreigners seem, at least to the English, to be intellectuals, this kind of thing should really help to stop them infesting the Sceptred Isle.

Of course, while you are pretending to be culturally dead, you will have to deal with the English. For those who are not anthropologists, Ken Livingstone of Brent East, my own Member of Parliament, has a description of his fellow-countrymen. He sees them as

> Really screwed-up, anally retentive, angst-ridden self-loathing, awful people.[19]

He adds:

> Xenophobia runs very deep in England. The Anglo-Saxon cultural heritage is not one we should wish to preserve.

Our intending visitor might question whether there is any point in going to Britain at all, when such an august personage as our Ken can say:

> I feel European. Whenever I'm in Europe I feel much more relaxed and at home.

Mr. Clement Attlee, a now not often remembered socialist Prime Minister of Britain, once told me that he thought foreigners were scared enough of the British not to come here in great numbers. This, Clem believed, was because they classified themselves in ways which produced derision in England. For instance:

> Europeans want to know what you DO
> Americans want to know what you HAVE
> The British, on the other hand, want to know WHO you are.

'You see,' said Attlee, 'You are supposed, in England, not to do anything. This is a hangover from the example of the landed gentry. As to what you have, it is extremely rude to ask anyone that. So a foreigner, on the whole, cannot open his mouth without being thought a bounder.'

I asked the former Prime Minister about the matter of 'who'.

'Well,' he said, with that strange grin on his face which was his trade-mark, 'people should always know WHO you are'.

15

Joining the Third World

Yesterday I travelled on a train destined for
Edinburgh. Being hungry and with a long
journey ahead of me, I went to the buffet car
and asked for a full English breakfast. I was
told I would have to wait for a gentleman to
finish his breakfast as there was only one fork
on the train.
    − Letter to the Editor of *The Independent*[1]

Of all the great secrets which I have managed to tease out of the
culture during my studies of more than forty years, none is more
amazing or more compelling than the one which I am about to
share with you. It will be of inestimable value to those few English
people who don't already use it to deal with foreigners, and
perhaps even more to those foreigners who are working on an
old, now superseded, model-image of the Brits. The discovery,
like so many great discoveries, was an entirely accidental one.
I stumbled across it through experience, not during deliberate
research.

I had been reading, for some years, the daily newspaper
accounts of police corruption; of people in very high places
carrying on very low practices; of violent demonstrations, the
breakdown of law and order, and so on. On top of that, I had
recently been importuned for tips, bribes, beer-money, 'a drink',
to 'see people right', reciprocal favours and the like, in connexion
with several transactions.

There was one particularly blatant incident, here in Britain,
once so well known for probity, rectitude and the rest. I suddenly
found myself saying, to a senior official who was taking all this
in his stride, 'I may have got away from the Third World,

126

but it has certainly caught up with me here!'

Then it struck me with thunderbolt force. Of course: this is how the British had solved their problem of being divested of empire, hegemony, moral ascendancy — and the things that their Press continually complains about. They had done an about-turn: they now behave almost exactly like the inhabitants of a Third World ('Emergent') country.

With trembling fingers, I wrote a list of indicators. They were all there — exactly as described by the once-judgmental British guardians of moral values — the hallmarks of a Third World country. It may or may not be useful to list them all, but within a few minutes I had a skeleton of the diagnostic.

Third World countries, Emergent/Developing Nations, were (and still are) most usually accused, *inter alia*, of the following twelve major faults:

- Police brutality and corruption.
- Absurd remarks by politicians and/or supposedly educated people.
- Human/legal rights denied.
- Ridiculous projects and/or political chicanery.
- Self-glorifying inflation of names, titles, occupations.
- Treating authority with derision.
- Ineffective technology.
- Sale of university degrees.
- Sale of nationality, residence, etc.
- Country becoming, effectively, a theme-park.
- Irresponsible, hysterical, destructive Press.
- Authority-figures/important/successful people, allegedly engaged in degenerate, corrupt or criminal behaviour.

If you don't recognise here the disaster of the Poll Tax; the Guinness and a dozen other affairs, the daily tabloids, the rat-catcher who is now a Rodent Operator, the cancelled or useless 'defence' equipment, the attacks on the Royal Family — then you should read more newspapers.

The outdoing of the Third World has become such a national passion that the newspapers are full of long-running stories about it.

Local currency not trusted in developing lands? How about this story from 1992:

> NO CONFIDENCE IN POUND SO FIRM PAYS STAFF IN MARKS
> Workers at a Leicester firm are to be paid in Deutschmarks plus a bonus from profits in currency deals.[2]

Of course, German marks are a hard currency, and a Third World country might be expected to pay in kind, so the comparison, it might be said, is not complete. Now, if you were to say that workers were paid in cocoa-beans ...

The *Daily Telegraph* can oblige:

> Cocoa beans are being paid to workers at three British factories. The 350 employees of Presbar Diecastings of Manchester and Britton Plastics of Birmingham and East Kilbride, Scotland, all owned by the Presbar Group, each earn around a fifth of a tonne of cocoa beans every week.[3]

Well, that might have been an accountancy dodge. But isn't that standard practice, too, in the Third World?

Bribery to obtain false papers? Surely not in England. But here we have:

> YARD CHECK ON PASSPORT RACKET
> A racket to supply illegal immigrants with British passports is being investigated by Scotland Yard ... it was suspected that fraudulent travel documents were in circulation on a fairly large scale.[4]

Surely such an important agency as the Passport Office is not badly organised, not the way one would expect in the Third World?

Well, according to one Member of Parliament:

> The administrative chaos which the Passport Office is in is providing golden opportunities for crooks and racketeers to make good profits.

Also profitable was the trade in driving tests.

> SCANDAL OF DRIVERS 'PAID TO PASS THE TEST FOR LEARNERS'[5]

Unscrupulous driving schools had been offering to hire impostors to take the test for clients in return for cash.

I have to admit that though still fairly far behind in many areas, on the whole the Ukkies have done a good job in imitating the Third World. Let a distinguished Englishman, the Queen's Counsel Anthony Lester, no less, speak for how things really are in the Sceptred Isle:

> [The United Kingdom] has been found guilty of more serious violations of fundamental human rights than any other European country . . . we are a deeply disunited Kingdom, especially in Scotland and Northern Ireland . . . we have an over-centralised system of government . . . our voting system is unfair . . . we have no code of civil rights and liberties to guide lawmakers, administrators judges and ourselves . . . we have been badly misgoverned by successive administrations that have treated us as subjects rather than citizens.

This picture of life as it really is in the UK may well be part of the Deterrence Mode. Surely many Third Worlders, coming up against the amazing anomalies of living in this country – especially when the facts of it are set out like this – must simply turn tail and flee.

Not least of these, surely, must be the large advertisement that appeared in *The Daily Telegraph*.[6]

At the top of a list of smaller ads for places like France, Spain and the USA, there is an 'OVERSEAS TRAVEL' offer. It is not for Patagonia, Malaga or Faro – but for the ENGLISH LAKES.

Is the *Daily Telegraph* Travel Offer trying to tell us something? Or is it attempting, in the Deterrence Mode, to deflect unwanted foreign tourists? And, just to make sure that you don't get lost, the four-day tour is 'Courier Escorted'. Does the presence of couriers mean that the place is dangerous, or difficult?

Third Worlders once sent their children, or themselves went to Britain, to get a better education than they could at home. They may or may not in future – if they read one past report of the independent National Commission on Education.[7]

It found that standards of literacy and numeracy in British schools were too low to meet the needs of a modern economy.

Of course, it all depends on what kind of a school you are looking for, as you can see from a report in *The Evening Standard:*

> 100 SCHOOLGIRLS RUN AMOK IN STATION
> BATTLE . . .
>   It was like a scene from an epic production of St. Trinian's, with a pitched battle raging between more than 100 screaming girls and police. It involved Convent girls and all.[8]

When it was over, five girls and a boy, all aged between 13 and 16, were under arrest.

At least developing countries are known for their quaint − if un-PC customs and sayings. Like this remark − by an employee of Essex County Council who was also a magistrate − concerning a case he was hearing:

> A woman, dog and a walnut tree,
> The more you beat them, the better they be.

The Oxford Dictionary of Proverbs is a rich store of adages which seem to suggest that a certain Third World outlook was perhaps once common in Britain. In embracing similar values today, the British can argue they are going back to their own ancient roots:

> Every Man Has His Price
> Love does much, money does everything
> A bribe will enter without knocking
> God help the poor, the rich can help themselves
> God help the rich, the poor can beg

And Oxford's

> What is it that gold cannot command, or hath not conquered?

is dated as far back as 1592; while the simpler, yet somehow authoritative *Money will do anything* is quoted from a source a generation earlier in 1563.

There was a time when cabinet ministers and others in high office who were caught out in something discreditable resigned immediately. The British, following several such incidents, threw the entire concept overboard in 20 to 25 years − thus showing at one and the same time pragmatism, economy of labour and a laudable reluctance to add to the unemployment figures. Not to mention solidarity with the Third World.

The British Post Office recently began to show the classic signs of Third World organisation: or should I call it behaviour? My first inkling came from the Inland Revenue. It sent me a warning recommending that I pay my tax bill directly through a bank. The Post Office, it seems, cannot be trusted to deliver mail safely any more.

Then *The Daily Telegraph* reported an experiment by trading standards officers in North Yorkshire, who were quoted 'six different prices to send identical packages'.[9]

Counter clerks were 'apparently baffled' by the pricing structure.

When I mentioned this test to a fervent (Estonian) defender of English ways, he snorted: 'That would be possible only in North Yorkshire.'

And yet, soon the papers were printing similar tales from all over the country. Someone advised the equivalent of the Third World haggle: 'take your parcel from post office to post office, and send it where the charge is lowest'.

Then there are the perennial rumours of Post Office privatisation. This too mirrors the Third World. Considering the tips and *bakhshish* needed in some countries to get a parcel from the clutches of their postal authorities, these are already privatised in all but name.

At least one can still rely on the banks over here. Although there have been running battles between some of them and customers claiming that their accounts were pillaged through foolproof wall cash-dispensers. One woman complained that when she asked for a £10 note to be changed, the bank teller tried to charge her £3 for the service.

In generating news which would not disgrace a Third World country, Britain keeps her end up well. One London newspaper has even claimed that a World War II bomber aircraft was found on the Moon.

And we are surely back to the good old Third World atmosphere with the High Court's ruling that MINISTERS ARE ABOVE THE LAW.

It is perhaps fitting that we are on this subject, for the case which elicited this interesting fact involved the deportation of a Zairean refugee. The court found no minister could be proceeded against in such a matter:

> The Home Secretary, and all other government ministers are above the law, the High Court ruled yesterday . . . The Home Secretary, unlike ordinary citizens, should be protected by a modern version of the divine right of kings.[10]

And you know those charming articles on foreign parts which adorn the travel pages of so many British papers? They contain marvellous experiences (when the writers can get away from barmen and taxi-drivers abroad). This kind of thing has, much to my delight, started to invade the ordinary news pages of the British Press:

> 300 BATS REVIVE DRUNKEN PATIENT
> tells of a hospital (surely worthy of the Third World) in Chippenham, Wiltshire, where a cloud of bats lived under the floorboards. They 'flew into the ward yesterday as a drunken patient was sobering up'.[11]

Every self-respecting Third World country has its wildlife: the bigger and fiercer the better. Until recently, it was thought that the only dangerous wild-cat in the Kingdom was the Scottish one. But it seems that Nature abhors animal vacuums as well as other kinds.

After rumours extending over many years, the British were at last to learn that the country had joined other developing lands with this headline:

> SCIENTIST CONFIRMS PUMAS ARE ROAMING BRITAIN
> 'The strange catlike creatures,' says the report, 'spotted in all corners of the British Isles are almost certainly pumas and lynxes that have escaped from captivity.'[12]

Dr. Paul Shuker, an authority on mysterious cats, actually keeps a stuffed jungle cat that was run down in Shropshire. 'Normally,' he says 'such animals are found in the Middle East and Asia.'

One catlike animal has killed hundreds of sheep, and the tracks of felines of this kind are said to follow the West Country patterns of deer migration.

Nor is that all. A llama was found on the railway line between Reading and Didcot, not so very far from London. And things reached a pitch a few years ago when a paper reported that a train had been delayed for the official reason that there were 'swans on the line'.

In the Third World, of course, it might have been 'buffaloes on the line'. There is very little difference, even in the exoticism of the idea. In, say, Asia, they might have been royal buffaloes. In England, since all swans belong to the Monarch, we have what might almost be called a close fit.

I even saw a letter from a newspaper reader saying how nice he found it that there should be such a pleasant obstruction as swans; or words to that effect. Even the victims of Britain's Third World policy, it seems, are pleased to get in on the act.

Large and small birds of prey are returning to breed in this country, after some time away. A Barbary lion has been exported from England to Morocco, where they have died out – and strange sea-creatures are joining those of the land and air.

Dr. David Holdich, of Nottingham University, says:

> The Turkish crayfish has become established in London . . . There is one 40-mile stretch of the Grand Union Canal in London where there are thousands of the creatures . . . during the hot summer, we had reports of them, 30 cms long, crawling out and onto the bank. As you can imagine, it gave people quite a shock.[13]

Perhaps hot-climate organisms are being encouraged by the Group Mind in anticipation of what seems like inexorable Global Warming? Concerned scientists and nature activists of all kinds are perturbed about the damage which it might do.

But news items in the British Press, with true Developing Nation optimism, argue that the apple crop could improve and sheep with thinner coats could be easier to shear, especially in northern parts of the British Isles, which are excessively damp and chilly as things are.

One might expect, of course, a hiccup now and then. Torquay's famous 'palm trees' were exposed as not palms at all, but the New Zealand cabbage plant. Bournemouth's were found to be little better: the City's own Parks Director described them as 'little Chinese lookalikes.'

I suppose that all is not yet lost, either for the tourist or Third World potential of the South Coast resorts of England, for I see that the *Sunday Express* has published directions for growing palm trees (via the airing-cupboard) from date-stones.

Ingenuity rather than misdescription lies behind many otherwise baffling British phenomena. Indeed, if the Brits were to realise it, their inventive capacity is really all they need. Concentrating on this potential would allow them to cease bemoaning shortcomings in other directions.

The old industries, which needed ingenuity to devise and to set up, have often collapsed or fallen into the hands of foreigners. Car-making, textiles, shipbuilding, even heavy construction – formerly the pride of developed countries – are now seen to be better suited to low-tech places.

But ingenuity still springs eternal. British computer programmers are the best in the world, they say. Ingenuity: there is plenty of sand in Arabia – but British firms are supplying English sand for filtration purposes there.

Tropical fruit? A plant laboratory in Glastonbury, Somerset, has developed British banana plants – and is selling them to Yemen.

It is known throughout the world that Britain has, for instance, the best crime-writers and the most ingenious murderers in the world. The more usual emphasis tends to overlook the ingenuity-content of this fact.

The English are not easily panicked. In fact, a remarkable picture is now emerging of the British as not only Third World, but also post-Third-World. For instance Mr. M.K. Whaler, of Hayling Island, Hampshire, wrote to the Editor of the *Sunday Telegraph*, with an interesting revelation:

> I notice from the most recent Royal Navy Broadsheet that there are a total of just 17 captains in command at sea.
>   Supporting them are 42 admirals (45 if one includes the apothecaries).[14]

Gilbert and Sullivan might have done better, but perhaps only a little. Two point-four admirals to control each captain. Or, perhaps, two admirals with eleven reserves . . . What happens if two admirals fall out, one wanting his ship to go one way and the other another? Perhaps the eleven extras could mediate.

And, hard on the heels of *that* news, came tidings from the House of Commons Defence Select Committee:

> the British Army . . . has one general for every two battalions. Not to be left out of it (there has always been rivalry between the various arms) the Royal Air Force has a whole air marshal for each squadron of its aircraft.[15]

Another example of the Post-Third World? Well, metals, particularly heavy ones, as we all know, pollute the earth and cause diseases. Third World countries should be discouraged from developing their polluting industries for this reason. So far, so predictable. Then, in 1992 came the headline in a normally politically-correct newspaper:

BRITAIN THRIVES ON DIET OF ARSENIC AND LEAD.

'How can this be true?' you and I — veterans of watching half a million definitive, if often wildly inaccurate TV documentaries — may cry.

Apparently Britain has not so much caught up with, but transcended the usual Third World rules. Scientists have discovered that for centuries pollution from mines has been poisoning soil on land now used for housing and farms. Yet locals appear to have suffered no ill effects. Arsenic, cadmium, lead, zinc and others — all the *bêtes noires* of right-thinking conservationists — are involved:

> Ancient tips have been festering for centuries, and some have been transformed, unwittingly, into gardens and fields for grazing. In a few places, this metal waste now forms more than 1 per cent of total soil content. Yet the effect on home owners, and the buyers of local crops, appears to have been negligible.

And on top of that, we're told that the amount of land being used for the cultivation of organic crops is insufficient to account for the volume of 'organic' products on sale in the shops.

Before the downfall of the USSR, British diplomats, knowing something of the strange conflicts in the economy and technology,

were fond of referring to the Soviet Union as 'Upper Volta —
with rockets.' Living in Britain can give the foreigner a similar
feeling: the spread of Third World qualities, while Britain
continues to teach tidier countries what's really what.

Professor Iain Thornton, of Imperial College School of Mines
in London, was asked to investigate the metals pollution business.
He seemed to have no trouble in spotting the opportunity in the
situation:

> In the US, and in Europe, there is now considerable concern
> about the dangers that mineral pollution — particularly lead
> — poses to drinking water. For more than 200 years mine
> waste leaching has been going on in Britain, so we should
> be the perfect people to get the answer.

Could the pollution turn out to be a blessing in disguise? It
seems unlikely, but I cannot forget the words of my Albanian
courtier friend Adhem Kastrati all those years ago, when I asked
him what would happen if Britain went broke. 'They will find
oil or something.'

In Third World cultures natural disasters are often considered
to be the work of whichever deity is considered locally to be most
likely to take umbrage. Cause and effect are simply not viewed
the same way they are in the developed world — and accidents
are likely to be ascribed to the supernatural. Nothing like the
Church of England, of course.

> 'The Windsor Castle fire may have been divine retribution
> for the Synod vote for the ordination of women, Canon
> Terence Grigg, Rector of Cottingham, North Humberside,
> has told parishioners.
>
> '"No sooner has the Church of England made its decision
> on women priests, than we have a fire at the home of its
> Supreme Governor," he said. "The coincidence seems
> amazing."'

My Religious Affairs Adviser informs me, though, that the
Church perhaps ought to fear punishment for having priests. He
reminds me that for centuries after the start of Christianity there

was no priesthood, and believers were strongly opposed to the whole idea.

We've come a long way since then. At one point the Church even resorted to advertising on TV with the slogan: 'CHRISTMAS IS ENOUGH TO BRING ANYONE TO THEIR KNEES'. Perhaps they'd heard about research done at Leicester Royal Infirmary.

WARNING BELLS TOLL FOR RINGERS.
Bell-ringing can be fatal; 40,000 campanologists who toll the church bells each week run the risk of death, serious injury, dislocations, skin burns and abrasions. Deaths are not as rare as might be expected from an apparently harmless activity.[16]

Returning to our Canon, however, we discover he is not alone in offering bizarre explanations for things. Officials offer such excuses almost daily or, as they would put it, 'on a daily basis'. (The average Brit seems currently unable to say 'daily', or even 'annually'. They have to use the word 'basis' in the phrase. It is a sort of mantram for them.)

As for asinine explanations, one episode sticks in my mind. When a new design for bank notes was unveiled, there was a storm of protest that they were horribly ugly and almost impossible to decipher. With a straight face, the highest authorities informed the public that they had been made deliberately confusing to make people look closely at them so that forgeries might be detected.

Someone somewhere may have believed that; possibly quite a number of people did. But to me it looked very much like a case of being economical with the truth. I waited, like the snipers of my Afghan glens.

Sure enough, not too much time passed before an unobtrusive item appeared in the news:

This week [Mr. Graham] Kentfield, the Chief Cashier of the Bank of England, took the unprecedented step of announcing that it would be altering the appearance of a bank note in response to a public outcry. [He said] ... 'it is the first time we have made changes in a note in response to public demand'.[17]

If you have not guessed it by now, disorganisation is another thread that runs though the above topics. Disorganisation has been raised to an art-form — even a weapon in the hands of the Brits.

And this, conveniently enough, brings me to a prime example. An instance where we can see the twin theories of Third World mentality and disorganisation working together, stumbling along with little interference from logic.

Nowhere is it more obvious that one is in a developing country than in its institutions. Now lately, I have had to stay in hospital — and I realised this would be the perfect opportunity to field test both theories. How could a first-class hospital in the capital city of a major western country possibly live up to the stringent standards of disorganisation set by the Third World? In truth, I felt in my heart it would fail this stiff challenge, and my stay would be a model of dull efficiency.

The service kicked off in time-honoured Third World fashion. As is customary in any self-respecting sweltering dicatorship, I was first of all presented with a bill for medicines I had never received. When I took it to the reception area to complain, a stern attendant told me to sit and wait for my name to be called — notwithstanding my protestations that I merely wanted to deliver a letter.

Once admitted, I was told to administer my own medicine. When I did so, I was accused of 'breaking the rules'. The kitchens required me to predict the food I'd feel like eating a day in advance. And this duly appeared — exactly an hour after the time I had been asked to select.

In true Third World fashion, there were compensations. As a heart patient, I was, naturally, offered meals dripping with saturated fats. Sugar, alcohol and cooked-to-death meals were also abundant.

The right atmosphere was created by constant incursions of well-wishers visiting the wrong rooms and hordes of their children running about while the parents engaged in loud debates in Arabic in the corridors. In case I ever felt lonely, the bedside telephone constantly shrilled with voices from Kuwait, Abu Dhabi, Dubai. They seemed not to care they had dialled the wrong room, and insisted on chatting for hours.

When night fell, the visitors went away, but now it was the

turn of the nursing staff to provide the entertainment. Raucous peals of laughter emanated from their station at three in the morning. Inconsiderately, I shouted at them to be quiet. The noise subsided for a few minutes; but the nurses never really understood the concept I was trying to convey. Every time I wanted a moment's rest, I was obliged to howl again.

I was weary, but triumphant. My theory was holding up under the most harsh circumstances. How would they respond to humour?

I enquired whether perhaps they kept a herd of elephants in the room above my head. At the time I could hear emanating through the floor the unmistakable sound of big game stampeding.

The nurses looked severe. 'There is nothing but an operating theatre up there,' they insisted. It left me with a mental image of an entire rugby team being operated on throughout the night – perhaps they had been given too little anaesthetic and had decided to fight back.

My own doctor – an eminent consultant – seemed quite distressed when he discovered that 'nobody seemed to be in charge'. But my theory's finest hour came when – and I don't expect you to believe this any more than I did at first – a senior doctor there suggested that 'illness was caused by demons'. His rationale, (I was told) as a religious man, was that although the demons brought the bacteria, it was a divine dispensation which allowed modern medicine to deal with it.

His theology was surely as formidable as that of the Canon on the fire at Windsor Castle. Looking up national statistics, I note that British psychiatrists and medical practitioners have the greatest suicide rate of all occupational groups in the United Kingdom. Are the demons winning, or what?

It was entirely fitting that the hospital refused to let me out until I had paid in cash for my x-ray – in spite of the fact that they knew me quite well, and were even better acquainted with my formidable insurance policy.

When I mentioned the matter to an Englishman I know, he took it quite calmly, retorting that, in the Third World, there would not have been a hospital at all. This was particularly confusing as I had been discussing some of the many thousands of hospitals in the Third World at the time.

It all chimed in perfectly with the spirit of the North African hospital I once visited which refused to admit patients because they might dirty its beautifully-polished floors. For decades I had dined out on this experience. Now I do not have to travel anything like as far.

English readers who are tempted to suggest to people from developed countries that they can easily become Third World ones, should pause at this point, for I want to make it clear that things are never as simple as they seem.

Indeed, much of my purpose in this book is to show how amazingly clever the British are, to achieve what seems at first sight to be the impossible.

You need considerable experience before you can convert to Third World: it's not something that you do like adopting vegetarianism or North Sea gas. And the British have been experimenting for some time, that's for sure. Take the following facts:

- It was an Englishman, Colonel Teddy Stead who invented the Abominable Snowman, so that even the Tibetans believe in it now. That did not, however, stop the BBC from launching an expedition costing about £1 million to search for it.

- It was English travellers and scholars who thought up the idea of 'marriage by capture' and taught 'native' people to practise a mime of it.

- It was an English explorer who fantasised, and later made 'real' the idea of tribal blood brothers: based on fourth-form English boarding-school initiations. Longing for status, the British also devised the concept of 'honorary chiefdoms' for white men. (And trained people in what they love to call Remote Tribes − remote from where? − to carry these out.)

- It was English archaeologists who invented the 'Mummy's Curse' legends, about the Tutankhamun and other tombs, to keep thieves out.

- It was English people who originally ate the sheep eyes originally served at Arabian banquets only to show how fresh the meat was.

If you find the last point particularly incredible, look at this letter, from Mrs. G. Blake, to *The Daily Telegraph*:

> It was never meant to be eaten . . . On one famous occasion a British diplomat in Saudi Arabia in the twenties, not knowing the ropes and not wishing to offend, popped it into his mouth. Thereafter the Arabs served it to us as a tasty morsel, believing the customer was always right.[18]

Of course, as with many things British, there is a near-precedent to the eyeball-eating, performed by an Englishman long before the Arabs ever heard of it.

In *Augustus Hare's Journal* (4 June 1884) it is recorded that Oxford's first professor of geology, William Buckland, was shown the heart of Louis XIV by his friend the Archbishop of York, who had bought it in Paris.

Observing that he had eaten many strange things, but never the heart of a king, the Doctor took it out of its box and gulped it down.

Not bad for one little group of offshore islands, eh?

There are only one or two small areas that could be improved on. One is the spread of English, unusual in a Third World language (though Arabic and Spanish, both extensively used in emergent nations, are growing fast in speakership). But we can take comfort from Philip Howard's observation:

> Pronouncing English 'correctly' is a lifetime's work for a native. For a foreigner it is impossible.[19]

Rather like one of those obscure African or Asian tongues, what? But sounds which may seem barbarous to some of us, are quite acceptable to the English.

We could reform the spelling, to make English look a little more foreign or even Third World, instead of only sounding so, as at present.

I have in mind:

GZZ
DH
KS
KW

NG
NGK
TH
ZH
SK
And WAAH, among others.

These are all good English sounds, except that they are not properly written down. Hence this phrase:

I think that this is the ring that was exactly the one in question – which I have just heard on the radio – could be better rewritten as:

I think dhatt dhis izz dha ring dhatt wozz iggzakttli dha wun inn qwestchun.

Yes, far more satisfying, far more Third World.

16

Contrary to Expectation

Magistrates put a stop to a planned celebration
of St. George's day (April 23) because the
commemoration of the Patron Saint of
England was 'not regarded as an occasion'.
— *Daily Express*[1]

This is an age, in Britain, when debunkery is very much the in
thing. So it should not surprise anyone to read a considered
response some forty years later:

> Because the English wore the emblem and invoked the name
> of St. George as they murdered and plundered across Palestine
> at the time of the Crusades, the argument goes, our sainted
> soldier-patron should now be cashiered . . . there is a perfectly
> respectable case for St. George, and a nation which has lost
> an empire and not yet found a role had better hold onto its
> saint.[2]

You will note that, perfectly normally for the British, the
'perfectly respectable case' is not outlined or even summarised.

There couldn't have been that many English in Britain at the
time of St. George, anyway: he was martyred in AD 303, and
the Anglo-Saxons drove the Britons into Wales only in the fifth
century. There wasn't, in fact, any England in Britain then. It
was still on the Continent, in Hathaby, Schleswig-Holstein in fact,
where there is a place called Anglen still to show for it. The
Anglenites had almost certainly never heard of St. George.

Acting contrary to expectation is a British speciality. That may
include rewriting history, changing cherished attitudes — or
simply refusing to react the way one would expect.

I was excited to see Leslie Gardiner's article:

FINDING A MODEL WORLD IN THE LAND OF OUR ANCESTORS.[3]

Now, at last, someone had been to an earlier home of the English, in Denmark. Surely he would have something resonant to say about it and full of significance for Brits. First the lead-in, about the boat trip; then, thrillingly, 'At Esbjerg, all Jutland was laid out before us: the land our distant ancestors came from . . .'

And that was about it. Apparently the place was a bit of an anti-climax: 'Connoisseurs of noble prospects find little to enthuse about in this part of Denmark.'

I had to wait more than two years to get a further inkling about Anglo-Saxon origins, this time in an article in *The Independent*. Patricia Clough was our guide – to Anglen, Schleswig-Holstein.

Again somewhat contrary to expectation, these north Germans have kept up to date with their Englander cousins. They actually wear navy blazers and flannels, smoke pipes, and like English prints. None of these items was known when their forebears said goodbye to the Anglos. Is it in the genes, or is the Ukkie taste only a refined German one?

'Ah you're English – so we're related,' said one to Ms. Clough. And there is more. They 'drink tea endlessly, and see ghosts. They go in for Staffordshire-type pot dogs . . .'[4]

Now, back to the present day. First, however, I should warn those who don't already know it that the Brits are quite capable of moving the goalposts. The most conspicuous example of this is said to be the Clean Machine event.

Every one knows the railways are famous for not being able to get the trains to run on time. They cannot get the dead leaves off the line, especially in Autumn. The whole system grinds to a halt when the weather is bad. It is a sort of tradition, and was once famously characterised in the days of British Rail as 'the wrong sort of snow on the line.' The fares are widely expected to be extortionate, the seats filthy and the carriages ancient.

One day the 11.55 commuter train duly arrived at Temple Meads Station in Bristol. It arrived empty and left empty. Why? Because, of course, it was not only on time (which made all the waiting commuters think that it could not possibly be *their* train) but it was clean, new and not packed: which must have put the clincher on the matter for them.

> Accustomed to a tatty old diesel service on the 3-mile journey from Bristol to Severn Beach, they refused to believe the Sprinter was for them.[5]

Perhaps they had not been told? Well:

> Station staff announced the arrival of the train over the tannoy to alert waiting passengers that the train was, in fact, for them. However, the travellers stood looking at their watches as it pulled away.

The railways have long been a rich source of contrary-to-expectation behaviour. Some years ago, *The Evening Standard* informed its readers that there were two conflicting images of rail travel . . .

> a svelte . . . waitress serving the traditional 'Inter-City Sizzler' breakfast to punters on the Paris-Brussels express, and a Manchester engine-driver who delays his passengers for five minutes while he plucks a pheasant on the platform.[6]

I rather like *The Standard's* final paragraph to this item: perhaps it encapsulates the contemporary British attitude:

> The first represents our yearning for efficiency and smartness; the second is the comic reality. Would we have it any other way?

So, if you are a foreigner, be warned. I can accept no responsibility for the double-bluff. Or, indeed, given the above example, the double-whammy either.

In its last days before privatisation, and besieged by complaints, British Rail resorted to desperate — and unexpected — measures.

LION OF RESISTANCE

A former lion tamer has been hired by British Rail — to handle irate passengers.

> Chris Jarvis, 46, now works in customer care at York station, dealing with passengers' complaints and problems.

He previously spent four years training lions and tigers at Windsor Safari Park's circus.[7]

The English child gets contrary-to-expectation training early: in fact, a current school book is reported by *The Economist* as teaching that

> 'Britain imports all its oil, London can communicate with Liverpool via a wireless link, and the pigmies are 'fierce little creatures but loyal subjects of King George V'.

Of course, the child may never have to learn the awful truth that His Majesty King George V is not now with us, or that the pigmies may well have PhDs nowadays, and be less fierce little fellows than hitherto, or even that Britain is a major oil-producing country. In which case, I suppose, there's no harm done.

I must admit to a touch of surprise, though, the other day. When I mentioned Delhi to a London chartered accountant, he started and said, 'I hadn't heard that they had changed the name from Delphi'. No, as I was careful to ascertain, in my methodical foreign way, it wasn't a joke. I expect he had been to a school where a certain kind of book is still being used.

Come to think of it, this sort of thing might just be the ideal weapon to use against foreigners. After all, how could they deal with it?

And it might make a good come-back when asked, for the thousandth time when you are on holiday 'Is England in London, or London in England?'

Perhaps the English should try it: 'Tell me, is Paris in France, or is France in Paris? Is Rome in Italy? I always thought that Italy was in Rome. Japan? That's in Tokyo, isn't it?'

Let us now turn to facts rather than speculation. Most Americans I have met seem to know the one about how many Poles it takes to change an electric light bulb. They may be gratified to hear that changing light bulbs probably now takes only one person in England, in one city, anyway. Though not before appropriate procedures were adopted.

The Daily Telegraph stated:

TENANTS IN DARK OVER LOSS OF A LIGHT DUTY

[Sorry about that: British newspapers simply love puns in headlines, evidently the weaker the pun the better]

Council tenants in Hull may be left in the dark for up to 72 hours until caretakers have been properly trained in the fine art of changing electric light bulbs ... light bulb maintenance does not form part of their job description ... Mr. Stephen Brindley, council housing director, is now proposing that caretakers be given special training in the changing of light bulbs.[8]

Of more serious inconvenience to foreigners may be the destination of their telephone bills.

£163 PHONE BILL SENT TO A MANHOLE

British Telecom has sent a £163.92 phone bill to a manhole on the A4095 near Bampton, Oxfordshire. The mystified postman delivered it to the nearest letterbox, at a nearby hotel.[9]

Contrary-to-expectation can kick in anywhere. I used to meet an English gentleman, whom I first encountered sitting on a bench on Hampstead Heath. He was always well-dressed, drove a BMW, lived in an exclusive part of north London, and was a regular attender at his synagogue.

His ambition, in fact, was to be well thought of by his fellows, to be a regular Saturday attender, 'wearing my three-piece suit and sitting among the successful businessmen.'

I didn't ask him what line of business he was in, and he never discussed it. We used to take our walk, it seemed, at about the same time, and ended up on that bench. Then, one day, seeming to be in an unusually communicative mood, he asked me to go with him on a business day out, covering 'a number of my outlets in Surrey'.

He brought a picnic and a rather heavy briefcase, which I assumed contained his samples, or his stock, or whatever visiting businessmen carry about in Surrey.

The first stop was at an idyllic, rustic hamlet with an archetypal village church.

'Just a moment.' He left me in the car. I must admit that when he came out rubbing his hands and murmuring, 'managed a good six months' worth there,' I wondered exactly what commodity was being negotiated.

We visited church after church — or, rather, vicarage after vicarage. My friend always returned to the car with some such enigmatic remark as 'I'll just make a note . . . send on by mail, emphasise continuity'. Once I thought I had got the drift, when Mr. Isaac Samuels muttered, 'Why didn't they tell me he was dead, to avoid embarrassing the relatives?' Evidently, I thought, he was some sort of insurance salesman.

As you will know, it doesn't do in England to be too inquisitive. In fact, ideally, you should never ask anyone anything at all. But there I was, a detribalised Afghan, in the leafy glades of rural England, becoming more and more perplexed.

'Are you in insurance?' I heard myself asking Mr. Samuels. He grinned. 'Sort of. Of course, it's my clients who are really in the insurance business.'

'Vicars?'

'That's right.'

Perhaps it was something . . . improper or illegal. Of course, I could not think that there was any law, even in England, against men of the cloth selling insurance. It was just that I had never heard of it before.

It was then that he made me undertake not to tell anyone while he was still alive, and I have kept that pledge, since he died three months ago. After extracting the promise from me, Mr. Samuels handed me a briefcase while he drove to the next appointment. He invited me to look inside.

It was full of photocopied sermons, with titles like:

SIDELIGHTS ON THE BVM
WHAT CHRISTMAS SHOULD MEAN TO US

and

MY REDEEMER LIVETH

I turned in the passenger seat and started to stammer 'But, but . . .'

'Yes', said Mr. Samuels, 'I thought it would surprise you. I'm a writer, just like you. *AND* I've got a pretty good market for my stuff, you know. Been at it twenty years.'

Always anxious to learn from the English, I considered for a wild moment asking whether my local synagogue could use an experienced writer. But then I realised that, with twenty years' start, Mr. Samuels probably had it sewn up already.

When I got home that day, I decided to give British research a rest, and soon immersed myself in a riveting autobiography. It was *A Sparrow's Flight*, by Lord Hailsham[10], one of the country's most intelligent and respected politicians and equally distinguished as Lord Chancellor.

The book fell open at a page 181 which described the various sects of the Lebanon and Syria. It included many briefings and copious notes about local men and matters which his work there involved in the 1940s.

My eyes fell upon a passage which states that the Alawites were 'until recently ruled by the Old Man of the Mountains (Sheikh el Gibal)'.

Until recently. It is widely known in the Middle East that the followers of the so-called Old Man were defeated and suppressed by the Mongols as long ago as AD 1256. Lord Hailsham's 'recently' was at least 695 years before he went there.

This was extraordinary, even by the standards of the East (Afghans, for instance often consider my family Arabs since we arrived in Afghanistan only in the twelfth century). Coming from an Englishman, such time-encapsulation is utterly unexpected.

To relate this anecdote to the associations of some at least of my foreign readers, I should mention that this was during the reign of Henry III. His father, King John, is reputed to have offered to become a Muslim, under the suzerainty of the Sultan of Morocco. His uncle, Richard the Lionheart, also spent much time in the East. Lord Hailsham is a pillar of the Established Church in the UK, but perhaps he is a reincarnation of an ancestor with similar affinities.

Just to be even more contrary to expectation, I expect, the author gives us an Egyptian Arabic form for the name of the Assassin ruler. To wrap things up, he insists that the language is standard Arabic, which, however, lacks a letter G.

There may be an even deeper secret here, of course, known only in the higher echelons of Britishness. Since it seems unlikely that the writer in such cases actually *could be* unaware of the facts, the whole thing is probably a ploy.

Or at any rate a mere form of modesty. Not wanting to be

thought a boaster, or to be parading knowledge, the British person goes so far as to appear ignorant, sometimes even grotesquely so.

It would explain why British Middle Eastern experts, including some who have spent years in the East, often seem to know next to nothing about the place. For instance, the reviewer, who has lived in and written about the Middle East, who claimed that the famous author and traveller Dame Freya Stark founded the Muslim zealot Brotherhood. That organisation was actually established well before her time by Sheikh Hasan al-Banna.

In fact, it was the comical 'Brethren of Freedom' which she ran from Cairo. It could not have been a more different outfit: an Allied propaganda effort which deceived nobody, but provided good teas at Groppi's café.

Even the newspapers may be in on it. They regularly mention a *fatwa* as a 'death sentence', whereas it is only a legal opinion. They call a Caliph a king, and a Gulf fisherman who has found oil 'a sheikh' and extol his non-existent lineage. They use Persian, Turkish and Urdu words indiscriminately for such things as coffee, veils and domes.

The Times seems to think that the title of the late King Hasan of Morocco was 'Amin al-Mouminine', and that this means 'descendant of the Prophet Muhammad'.[11] This notwithstanding that it is in fact something very different (Emir al-Mu'minin). Or that it really means 'Commander of the Believers'. Peculiarly, the paper transliterates the words in the way used in French. And it encourages readers to accept this nonsense by datelining the story 'Amman' — an Arab capital.

The same paper, in common with virtually every section of the British Press, insists on believing that *jihad* means *Holy War*. Of course, as any Muslim will tell you, the word means 'struggle', and all Muslims are deemed to be engaged in a struggle of right against wrong. Indeed, the Prophet himself is reported to have said, after a military campaign: 'We return from the lesser Jihad to the Greater Jihad.'

As if triumphantly to confirm my suspicions that more is going on in the British mind than foreigners will ever be able to fathom, here is a piece in *The Independent*. Ms. Sue Gaisford, in the course of a brilliantly entertaining piece of reportage, records the reactions of a British couple to the splendours of Istanbul. Sitting behind her in an air-conditioned coach, surrounded by the seething sights and sounds of this amazing city, are they impressed? Confused? Enthusiastic about the strangeness of it all?

Not a bit of it. Contrary to what would have been my own expectation, the husband is interested in the pigeons:

'Look,' he said, 'there's a scruffy little one over there. Must be a poor relation, I expect. My word, they've certainly got problems with their pigeons over here.' His wife agreed, adding wearily: 'All these mosques − competition between the vicars, I shouldn't wonder.'[12]

Could you beat that? The nearest I have got was when I asked the landscape designer Russell Page to send me his impressions of Morocco. Being English, he produced this message:

Everything is rather confusing, because most Moroccan waiters look like British cabinet ministers. On reflection, I realise that most English ministers look as if they should be Moroccan waiters.

Page was a non-drinker, and could not have been influenced by the heat of the sun, since he visited Morocco in winter. Contrary to expectation was something he took about with him, and applied to others as well as, very possibly, practising it himself.

British newspapers are full of solecisms and passages absolutely contrary to expectation. A random example is the letter from a distressed correspondent in France. Advice in *The Times* that French women be addressed as *'mon amiante'* galvanised the agonised Frenchman to protest:

'The word in French happens to mean asbestos'.[13]

The British, as always, have it both ways. They are patriotic, modest and self-effacing, and can be self-flagellatory to a degree perhaps inconceivable elsewhere. For instance:

THE BRITISH ARE ALL BARK AND NO BITE
We are champion grumblers. Grumbling is the self-indulgence of the masochist, whose ultimate grievance would be to have the cause of his grievance removed . . . Our world supremacy was just a wink in time's eye. In reality we are underlings.
We let the Romans take over our country, and make us

bow the knee in Latin. Then we let the Normans take over
our country and bow the knee in French.

Lord Macaulay, fulminating about how shamefully easy
it was for French tyrants to make slaves of English villeins
was very good on this: 'The subjugation of a nation by a
nation has seldom, even in Asia, been more complete.' ...

We are not citizens, we are subjects ... [we] relapse,
grumbling, into a corner of the kennel.

Good dog.[14]

Of course, if we recall our teaching by the Central European
psychiatric schools, we can always turn such sentiments to good
account. According to such theories, everything can mean the
reverse. So, if you prefer, these statements may really be
affirmations of *superiority*.

17

Mr. Thomas's Fruit

News report in the *Enfield Advertiser*:

Dead pensioners are depriving taxpayers of thousands of pounds — because they have not sent their bus passes back.

— *The Daily Telegraph*[1]

In the Lebanon, one day someone took an English gentleman — a Mr. Thomas — a present of delicious cactus fruit. Mr. Thomas, perplexed at the number of seeds, removed them all. The result? No fruit remained.

Something tasty but perplexing, or something which just doesn't add up, is now widely known in the East as 'Mr. Thomas's Fruit'.

I once asked at the British Council library in Beirut what information they had about any Mr. Thomas who had resided there. Happily, there was a trace: 'After leaving Beirut, he went to Shanghai, where he taught Mandarin dialect.'

This may be slightly irrelevant, but it does resound curiously with other British careers abroad. A UK teacher of classics (Greek and Latin) in Cairo returned home and before too long was a professor of Classics (Persian) in England. More recently, *The Daily Telegraph* noted this about Professor D. M. Dunlop, the noted Orientalist:

During the 1939-45 War, he served in the National Fire Service and afterwards lectured in Semitic languages at St. Andrews University.

Britain is the spiritual home of the Mr. Thomas Fruit. The

tradition is well maintained in smaller publications; and *The Daily Telegraph* is adept at finding examples. As well as the extract which heads this chapter, the DT unearthed this one from *Reform*, the monthly magazine of the United Reform Church:

> 'A pilot educational course is designed to enable funerals to become more satisfactory occasions both for the deceased and bereaved.'

There is no equivalent that I know of in English, but I would call a Mr. Thomas's Fruit situation that in which a certain section of British society found itself:

SHEPHERDS FAIL TO JOIN THE FOLD.
    An attempt to give shepherds, shepherdesses, stockmen and women professional status, with private health care and a graduated career structure, has failed.
    The Professional Herdpersons' Society says it has attracted only 51 members since it was launched last year – it had hoped for 10,000 – and is to be wound up.[2]

As in the case of the Fruit, the content was outside the container.

History, or folklore, does not record what Mr. Thomas said or thought when the fruit ceased to exist before his eyes. And, the more I live in Britain, the more I tend to think that he took very little notice of it. At the most, he may have described it as: 'the fruit disappeared . . .' Now look at two Press reports. One tells us that CLERGY ACCEPT BIBLE MIRACLES; the other CHURCH 'FECKLESS' IF IT HEEDS CHRIST'S WORDS – the first-named is from a poll by The Church Society. The second quotes the Church's own counsel, the QC Mr. Robert Walker, in the High Court. Indeed, he even used the words 'Christian fecklessness'.

Like Mr. Thomas, I note that something seems to have vanished before my eyes.

But what could it be? In the early nineties, His Royal Highness the Prince of Wales was quoted as criticising the religious tradition of which he was due to become the Supreme Governor. He resented, we are told, the 'overbearing and domineering attitude towards God's creation of the Judeo-Christian heritage'.

Does that mean that he approves of something other? Yes – he: 'praises Islam, while finding harsh words for the Bible'.[3]

'Everything in Britain cancels everything else out,' was the way the American Ambassador Kennedy, father of President Kennedy, expressed it to someone when I was once, as a curious teenager, eavesdropping on their conversation. But I must say I prefer the Mr. Thomas tag.

Especially since the Ambassador, who unlike me was rather hostile to the Brits, added: 'Britain is God's way of showing the world how NOT to live!'

Still, they do say in my neck of the woods that there are thousands of ambassadors in heaven – and millions of them in hell.

Oddly enough, and perhaps more often than Ambassador Kennedy would have liked, things *do* seem to cancel each other out in Britain.

Consider this:

> Last week's mortar attack at Crossmaglen, which injured a civilian, has had an unexpected bonus for the Army. The base's central heating has been ineffective for some time and the cost of repair was estimated at £8000. The explosion has shaken the dirt out of the pipes and the heating is now perfect.[4]

I gather that the Japanese do not have a handy equivalent to our Mr. Thomas rubric. I say this because an infuriated Tokyo professor has written to me, having read *The Natives are Restless*. He complains about something composed by Samuel Wilberforce, Bishop of Winchester (I did not, incidentally, use the quotation). He thinks that I should include it in a future edition, and 'correct the Bishop'.

If he means the last point literally, he should be informed that, since the good Bishop's dates are 1815-1873, I lack the necessary delivery contacts. But here is the poem that caused offence:

If I were a cassowary
On the plains of Timbuctoo,
I would eat a missionary,
Coat and bands and hymn-book too.

Analysed by the formidable Oriental academic (a teacher of English) and somewhat compressing his narrative, it transpires that:

- A cassowary (Malay word) is found in New Guinea, not in Africa.

- It is vegetarian, and could not kill or eat a missionary.

- Timbuktu is a town in Africa and has no plains.

- A missionary would not be wearing a 'coat and bands', as African missionaries, especially in the searing climate of Timbuktu, do not.

- Missionaries are forbidden by law in the area, so there would be no prayer-book, either.

He does not deny, however, that there is a place called Timbuktu (his spelling) so I suppose the Professor's Thomas Fruit residue equals − Timbuktu.

The debate surrounding the establishment of a British National Lottery may be viewed as a prime example of the phenomenon I choose to call 'Mr. Thomas's Fruit'.

During the campaign for a lottery, public scruples were overcome by appeals to their greed culture and money. For instance, it was pointed out that the British Museum, of worldwide repute, was built from the proceeds of a lottery. Good causes would benefit. If that were not enough, the prize would be a million pounds a week or thereabouts.

However, when it announced how the great event would be organised, the Government stressed that the 'very British lottery ... would avoid appeals to greed'.

So, like Mr. Thomas's fruit, the greed − whether for culture or money − was subtracted. The only thing left was, I suppose, the prospect of a million pounds and the good works that would be done with the profits.

But should the Government not perhaps remove the possibility of greed? It could, for example, spend the winner's prize-money on good works instead of exposing him or her to temptation.

Oddly enough, in Afghanistan, another tale involving a Briton has given rise to an organic simile − in much the same way as the story of Mr. Thomas and his fruit has done. It concerns a Mr. Crawshaw who had a peach-tree growing out of his head.

When questioned about the utility of this (barren) growth, he is said to have replied, 'It may seem bizarre to you, but look at the wonderful shade it gives!'

Mr. Crawshaw's tree − which in Afghanistan has become a term for an absurd or manifestly untrue explanation − is alive and well in Britain today. Fritz Spiegl, in a delightful piece in *The Listener* could have been addressing this very subject:

A Vicar, arrested the other day, explained that he was accosting prostitutes only so as to try to convert them . . . 'I only wanted to talk to them' figured frequently in proceedings arising from picket-line violence. Burglars caught in someone's backyard usually explain away their jemmy and gloves with the stock excuse, 'I was looking for my cat'. And you'd be surprised how many 'innocent bystanders' during the fashionable urban riots a few years ago carried half-bricks. They were all 'on me way to see me gerl-friend' − usually at 4 am.[5]

There is still scope, among the British, for a name for something which is not what it seems. I have just noticed, for instance, an advertisement for a 'fragrance for men' (which means a scent) which is said to be 'evocative of England's green and pleasant land'. Among other things, it contains 'spices and citrus' − both, of course, well-known British products.

Similarly, craving fish the other day, I was surprised to discover at my local supermarket, packages labelled 'cod's loins'.

I have thought for a considerable time that there should be a non-judgmental simile for terms such as German silver, Bombay Duck, American cloth, and the rest, which have really nothing to do with the things they purport to be.

Again, perhaps, we might name the Jackson Problem after

Mr. Anthony Jackson, who lowered his garden wall, and got into trouble for it. *The Daily Telegraph* says:

> A businessman who contravened ancient monument rules when he lowered a garden wall at a medieval ruin was fined £3000 yesterday.[6]

Just so; surely medieval monuments should be protected, even if they are ruins. The miscreant was also required to pay costs of £894 at Bury St Edmunds Crown Court.

The castle, in whose grounds Mr. Jackson's house was built, dates from the 13th century. When was the wall built? 'Although the wall was built in the 1930s, it was protected.'

Nineteen-thirties? Mr. Jackson wanted to take some of the modern wall down so that he could see his garden. 'To suggest it was part of an ancient monument was "plainly ludicrous"'

Now, I must declare an interest in modern garden walls. Perhaps I'd better phrase my account carefully, for I am obviously not as *au fait* with Britain as I should be. The facts are as follows:

Here in London, a few days ago, I had the temerity to have mounted a trellis on my front garden wall. Within 24 hours the authorities were at my door, commanding me to remove it or else. Not only did I need planning permission, but I would never, never, get it. Put up a 2-metre trellis on top of a (modern) wall? Preposterous. Naturally terrified, I promised to remedy the situation. Does anyone want an unused trellis, very expensive when bought, 2 metres by 6 metres, unsuitable for garden walls?

Mr. Jackson had been warned, by the police, no less. The words of the Recorder at Bury St. Edmunds Crown Court are still ringing in my ears:

> 'Nobody had clearer warnings than you. Your arrogance is beyond belief.'

For me, at least, the story had a happy ending. Inquiries ascertained that, while no trellis could be placed on top of the wall, a moveable screen − such as privet hedges in tubs, which performed exactly the same function − was entirely acceptable.

I am particularly glad I didn't try to lower what garden wall there is on the site of the ill-fated trellis. It looks suspiciously 1930s to me.

18

Doublethink or Doublespeak?

> We arc not at war with Egypt: we are in armed
> conflict.
> — British Prime Minister Anthony Eden

All British people reserve the right to change their minds, to deny
that something is (or was) so, or otherwise to alter what the rest
of us take as reality. And they will brook no interference with
this right.

The most conspicuous general example is that of Parliament,
whose majority party will seldom, if ever, accept what has been
enacted by another administration. It also explains the inordinate
time it takes to ratify a treaty, the reluctance to sign declarations
of human rights, and so on.

But don't blame the politicians. If they are really elected to
express the will of the people, they are only reflecting British
attitudes when they refuse to commit themselves to anything for
long.

Poll after poll tells how people do not trust politicians, of
whatever party. This does not stop the electorate from voting
for them. Neither does it stop said politicians from claiming that
they represent the wishes of the people when they enact legislation
quite different from what they were elected for. Or from refusing
to enact legislation (whether a bill of rights or a restored death
penalty) which the electorate *do* want.

I have had to add a question mark to the title of this chapter
because nobody, including the British, yet knows very much about
the phenomena of Doublethink and Doublespeak. They seem to
cause what are increasingly known as U-Turns in speech and
policy.

It does not matter how brilliant you are. Senior ministers,

159

extensively billed as 'first-class brains' or 'high flyers' (by nebulous references to august authority, though nobody ever discovers who this is) constantly create havoc by contradicting themselves. The fact that they can be seen burbling nonsense on television nightly fazes nobody.

These are the first-class brains, as they are called. As my friend Peter Brent used to say, 'Perhaps it is as well that it is left to our imagination to guess what a second- or third-class brain might be like'.

But, as with so many things British, we must again ask: is the ambiguity deliberate or simply built into a thoroughly viable muddle-through process?

Whether this headline strikes you as bizarre, or perfectly adequate will almost certainly depend upon whether or not you are British:

> 'BLACK BASTARD' NOT RACIAL ABUSE, SAYS TRIBUNAL
> A black car worker's dismissal had led to a loss to car makers Austin Rover of more than £100 million, due to a strike. An industrial tribunal ... said it was no different to saying that someone was Scottish, Welsh or Asian and illegitimate ... not intended [that] there should be a racial meaning.[1]

It is this factor which enabled the Prime Minister, in 1956 when the British Army had attacked Egypt, to make that pronouncement: 'We are not at war with Egypt'.

What exactly, was the relationship? It was then that Mr. Eden kindly obliged by clarifying: 'We are in armed conflict'.

This, it must be admitted, is clearer than the euphemism employed for the Korean War. This was 'A Police Action', with its comforting mental image, for the British mind at least, of a panting Bobby in pursuit of a masked burglar with a sack marked SWAG.

Foreigners reading this probably think that I have made up these quotes. English people, and those accustomed to Anglean culture, will wonder, I expect, what I am making such a fuss about.

But I propose to pursue this a little further, along the muddle route. The School of Pharmacy at a Liverpool university tried to discover what common medical instructions actually *meant* to patients.

Told to avoid alcohol, only 45% of men under 20 years of age said that they thought it meant 'no alcohol at all'.

'With plenty of water' meant to 28.8% the same as 'a few sips'. People were really confused by 'so many times a day'. For some a day meant 24 hours, for others 12 or 18 hours.

'Avoid exposure of Skin to Direct Sunlight or Sunlamps' meant, for 25%, that they could go out in a T-shirt and jeans on a hot, sunny day. Nearly 10% 'thought they would still go outdoor swimming in similar weather'.

'Apply sparingly' meant to 28% who had just left the doctor's surgeries, 'apply a thick layer'; 8.5% thought that it meant 'apply in large amounts'. 22.8% imagined that the direction meant that the cream should be used 'regularly'.

Naturally, this being England, the prescribing doctors were found to think in a similar way to the patients. Doctors often either gave no instructions or wrote 'as directed' on the prescription.

And a *Which?* Magazine competition for 'Loopy Labels' on medicines, quoted by the *Institute for Health Sciences Journal* turned up some real stunners.

A man with both eyes inflamed by hayfever was expected to put 'one drop into the *left* eye'. A woman was given a bottle of pills, and instructed on the label to 'take one half an hour *before* the onset of pain'. The label on a preparation which a man had been told to paint on an anal fissure read 'Paint liberally on the *arms*'. [my italics]

Foreigners should note at this point that, fortunately, in the same issue of the *Journal*[2] it is noted that Lincoln Crown Court has ruled that FORK-EATING IS NOT INSANE. This follows a case where a man who had swallowed a great deal of cutlery was adjudged sane by the court 'on the advice of a psychiatrist'.

Whether anyone had examined anyone in the Court (presumably the psychiatrist had been vouched for, in the usual manner, by being analysed by his peers before being allowed to practise) was not recorded.

Doublethink/doublespeak can come into its own in a big way

with newspaper headlines, showing once again that anything can mean something or its exact opposite, among the Brits. Try a few on for size:

BRITS FLEE ETHIOPIA AS REBELS CLOSE IN
Scores of Britons joined a mass exodus from Ethiopia yesterday ... (*The Sun* 27 May 1991)

BRITS SNUB WAR ALERT — Most of the 400 Britons in war-torn Ethiopia yesterday ignored Foreign Office advice to leave. (*Mirror* 27 May 1991)

Then there is:

The Times: FEWER APPLYING TO BE FAST-STREAM DIPLOMATS

and:

The Daily Telegraph: UPSURGE IN WOULD-BE AMBASSADORS

The Times tells us that 'Highly qualified young people are no longer flocking to join the diplomatic service'.

Disappointed? Never mind: *The Daily Telegraph* can refute this instantly, and from the same source[3], with: 'The lure of the diplomatic service is growing ... more than 2,200 people, mostly recent graduates, applied last year for 25 posts in the Foreign Office "fast stream".'

It is perhaps more understandable, to a foreigner, that some papers might want to encourage investment. Then we would get:

HOUSE PRICES ARE GOING UP AGAIN (*Daily Mail*)

Then, again, investment might respond better to suggestion on the same day in the *Telegraph*:

HOUSE PRICES FALL.

And, finally, two headlines on the same day in 1992:

CHEWING GUM 'DOES NOT STOP TOOTH DECAY' — (*The Independent*)

and:

GUM CAN HELP CUT TOOTH DECAY – (*The Times*)

I will spare you quotes from my collection which show both that the British are happy and that they are sad, that they are prosperous and broke, that they like foreign travel and detest it, that they are healthy and sickly . . .

This doublethink expertise may well lie behind the fondness the British have for stories and jokes about misunderstandings and equivocation.

A Swedish Professor, from a nation seldom regarded by the British as extravagantly romantic thinkers, was dining at my house one evening. He arrived late, and in a state of some psychological disarray. 'The British amaze me!' he muttered.

When he was a little restored and eating, he regaled us with his adventure. Visiting a colleague whose name and approximate address he had been given, he found himself near one of those multi-storey apartment blocks built by London councils.

A boy of about eight was bouncing a ball in the forecourt, and the Swedish professor asked him if he knew the apartment of Dr. Larsen. Yes, he did. Could he show it to him? Of course.

But, as not infrequently happens, the lift was out of order.

The Swedish Professor and the small boy puffed their way up twelve flights of stairs. The boy pointed out a door. 'That's Larsen's place,' he said.

The Professor knocked and rang, but there was no answer.

'They're out,' said the boy. 'We passed Dr. Larsen going out as we started up.'

'Then why the devil didn't you tell me?' roared the Professor, thoroughly incensed.

'You didn't ask me, did you?' said the boy.

Whether this is true or not, I do not know; but the man was in such a state that something must have happened to him.

One example of equivocation, or is it double-think, which I can truly vouch for is the one involving my friend Peartree. I had given him a letter of introduction to an Afghan relative who I hoped would give a little hospitality to Peartree, a frequently-wandering intellectual, who was on a world tour.

Peartree set off, saying that he would be back in a couple of months. I didn't see my Afghan kinsman for a few years. 'That Peartree,' he said, 'knew hospitality when he met it.'

'How so?'

'He stayed with us for nearly a year. Outings, exhibitions, concerts, expeditions. Even came on holiday with us . . .'

'I *am* sorry,' I said; 'but couldn't you have hinted that it was time to move on?'

'That's exactly what I did do. I said, "Won't your wife and children miss you after all this time?"'

'What did he say?'

'He said: "How thoughtful! I'll bring them over right away!"'

'Then what?'

'Then he went to my travel agent, booked the five of them first-class tickets in my name — and they all stayed a further five months!'

19

The Foreignness of Foreigners

Having survived Paris half a dozen times, I can
say now that I think I'd prefer the lynch-mob.
— Neil Lyndon, in *The Times*[1]

It was Evelyn Waugh who spoke of Eric Newby's delight in the
'foreignness of foreigners'. To most people, of course, Britain
is the most foreign place they are likely to visit. A great deal
depends upon what one is used to.

An Afghan visitor, Gul Samandar, wrote the following extract
after arriving in London from his own, statue-less country:

There are images everywhere. Men on horses, sitting in
equestrianly impossible poses, wearing hats with cascades of
feathers; men striding along, as if about to walk over a cliff.
Men in terrible, outdated clothes — even dressed as Roman
emperors, though I don't really expect you to believe this.
Men making Masonic signs, standing or sitting with books,
manning guns, holding sticks, gazing out to sea. Some statues
are perched on buildings, others on plinths in parks, some
are in front of public buildings or around churches. Mostly
they are in terrible condition: green with copper-rot or worse.

It is impossible to know what effect they have on the hordes
of people who pass them every day: perhaps none at all.

British travel writing as a whole revels in the ways foreigners
insist on not being British: their dietary habits, mispronouncing
of English words, funny clothes, happy laughing peasants and
so on. I know one travel writer in London who makes a tidy living
doing this kind of thing for magazines. He has not, so far as he
will admit, ever left these shores. In fact, I am sure that he is
one of the early and unsung pioneers of the Study of Culture

at a Distance – he has been getting away with it for forty years.

But, as I was recently reminded, delight in foreignness need not be based on approval. *The Daily Telegraph* put it succinctly in a leading article:

> We *enjoy* hating and distrusting the French just as they enjoy reciprocating our sentiments, with interest.[2]

This may be meant jokingly; but it certainly fooled me, for the article also says such things as:

> A nation which still holds in high regard the Emperor Napoleon, who brought greater bloodshed and misery to Europe than any man before Hitler, commands our lasting disdain.

And there is more, much more, including:

> There seems no nationality with whom it is less advisable to be competing for a place in a lifeboat after a shipwreck than the originators of *sauve qui peut*.

When the French President, staying at Buckingham Palace, was reported to have dunked a croissant in his coffee, there was considerable delight. Everyone knew that the French were uncouth. A correction, printed low down, well past the middle pages of the papers, that this was standard practice in France, was probably largely unread.

Of course, in order to be perceived as foreign, one ought to show visible signs of foreignness. When I wrote *Kara Kush*[3], a novel about the Afghan resistance, and was interviewed on radio, the presenters constantly had to explain to their audiences why they could detect no foreign accent in my English. They made up the usual theories, telling their listeners that I had been to school in England or had had English nannies.

For a large part, English people do go by the speech of the foreigner. Germans they conceive as always saying *Ach, zo!*, which is supposed to be comical in the extreme; almost as funny as the French supposed '*Izz ziss zatt*?'

As an Anglophile, I forbear from saying (self-censorship is very common, a tradition really, in Britain) what the English sound like when attempting another language. If you really want to know, ask a Frenchman.

I was talking to an English admiral one day, when I mentioned something about being a foreigner. 'Why, man, you're as British as I am!' he rasped; 'You only have to open your mouth and I can tell that!'

Foreignness has become much more relative in recent years. How foreign one sounds and looks is taken into consideration. Not long ago, I was complaining about some overseas residents who were making a nuisance of themselves near my London house. The official to whom I spoke insisted that 'we must make allowances for ethnic customs like playing loud music and even ogling women. They mean no harm.'

'I said, 'I don't mean any harm, either. Besides, look at my face, look at my name. What about *my* ethnic rights? I am ethnic, too, aren't I?'

He gave me a hard look. 'Not ethnic enough, I'm afraid, mate,' he said.

But of course you can be British and *not* speak a word of English that your countrymen can understand.

ENGLISHMAN EXCUSED FROM SCOTTISH JURY said the headline, explaining that Adrian Roberts was called up for jury service in Edinburgh. He had been born in Sunderland and 'couldn't understand half of what people were saying'. The Court discharged him.[4]

So it isn't always the language: again we find one of the stranger features of Britain: that when something seems cut and dried it disappears, like the grin on the face of the Cheshire Cat.

For instance, Britain, after quitting the empire, was to rule Europe; was to reverse its failing fortunes by extracting oil from Tanganyikan peanuts; was to have nuclear electric power almost cost-free . . .

Among the many endearing habits of foreigners which cause British people to warm to them is their hospitality. They are generous, often from sparse resources, and offering to pay is treated as an insult.

In contrast, the corresponding lack of hospitality in British life takes the foreigner a while to get used to. It is still utterly baffling to many overseas visitors, except for those who visit the North.

Where else in the world, for instance (except perhaps parts of

North America where I suspect it started) would 'hospitality' mean something you pay for? As in 'enjoy the hospitality of the X Hotel ...'

And even British people (admittedly they were mostly from the countryside or Wales, Scotland and other peripheral areas) have complained about the 'before or after' habit. This, for those who are studying the culture at a distance, is when people say 'Do drop in *after* luncheon, will you?' or, 'We are having pre-dinner drinks'. Or even 'Let's see ... tea is at four; come at five, just before cocktail-time when we always visit the Bloggs-Fotheringays's, would you? We can fit you in for half an hour.'

There was recently a comic act at a Cairo nightclub which brought the house down. The pay-off line was an Englishman being told by an Egyptian: 'Yes, I'd love to reciprocate your hospitality. British-style, of course. Shall we say my place, one day during the fasting month of Ramadan, perhaps in ten years' time?'

The mournful Kuwaiti who told me about it said 'A joke like that is worth two regiments to Saddam Hussein.'

If you are a foreigner though, remember that cavalier treatment is not entirely reserved for you. Take this rather extreme example of how the British treat *each other*:

> Some friends who arrived recently for a high table dinner at Christ Church, Oxford, hung about in a freezing quad for an hour and a half before it became clear that their intended host was absent without leave.
>
> They found their way to the Senior Common Room, where a dishevelled academic consulted a list. He informed them briskly they were not on it. 'Oh dear,' they said. 'We shall just have to drive all the way home to Somerset.'
>
> 'Oh dear, so you will,' said this dreadful don, dispatching them into the cold night without so much as a thimbleful of sherry. The only person at Christ Church who showed them a morsel of kindness was the porter.[5]

I am not suggesting that the British are stingy by nature. Indeed, the very existence of a book teaching how to be mean seems to point the other way. It is called *Super-Scrooge: Your Time Has Come*[6] and costs a mere £5.95.

The British are given to regarding, in theory at least, the Scandinavians as closest to them in outlook. However even they are not above foreignness, and do uncalled for things like pressing food on you. One long, and generally well-balanced, article on Denmark, in *The Times* ends with 'I think I would go mad if I lived there'.[7]

And the Vikings, from whom many Brits are supposed to be descended? The York Archaeological Trust (York was founded, as Yorvik, by Vikings) reconstructed the face of an eleventh century Norseman.

Reproduced in a newspaper was a photo of this face, looking rather wimpish (I imagine he would, because he had probably just been murdered, an archaeologist told me). It was contrasted with a warrior-type photo of an actor.

Headlined IF THIS IS YOUR IDEA OF A VIKING, THINK AGAIN, it continues:

> He's slightly built, nicknamed Eymund, and hardly the type to rush around raping and pillaging.
>
> But it seems that this is what your average Viking really looked like. A wimp . . .
>
> Just 5ft 6 in tall, with wispy blond hair, he looked older than his twenty-something years.
>
> A far cry from the archetypal, granite-jawed, macho man depicted by Kirk Douglas in the 1958 film *The Vikings*.

That got at least one descendant of the Vikings' blood up. Wulf Hendriksen, sent the cutting to me, with this comment:

> You may care to note in any forthcoming writing that these wimps are the ones who frightened the English so much. If you recall, the English prayer was 'From the fury of the Danes, Good Lord, deliver us!' What kind of mice were the ones who were fearful of wimps of 5 feet 6 inches?

I must say that the reconstruction looks uncommonly like Kevin, our window-cleaner here in London. He is English: I cannot detect anything foreign about him, except his Taiwanese shell-suit, Korean trainers, German eye-glasses and Spanish bucket.

20

How Horrid IS *Abroad?*

British schoolchildren are totally lost when it comes to geography ... More than a quarter of 11-year-olds cannot find America or Russia on the globe; the same proportion makes a *faux pas* over France. One in six cannot even identify the United Kingdom.[1]

— *The Sunday Times*

'Abroad' really is abroad when viewed from Britain, in a way quite different to what it feels like observed from anywhere else.

And if Abroad is not like Britain, well, it should be.

Many in Britain, especially the higher echelons, behave as if everyone should be like the British. This is still true of the supposedly democratised fighting services.

For instance, shortly after the Gulf War, Kurds in northern Iraq, who are all Muslims and never touch the flesh of the pig, received relief supplies of food from the Royal Air Force — of pork luncheon meat and bacon-burgers. That should teach them to be less foreign.

I haven't heard anything so interesting since I saw the huge, beautifully-printed, colour poster issued for the Middle East by the then Ministry of Information in London fifty years ago.

It showed a smiling bedouin sheikh, in full Arabian rig, raising a tankard of frothy beer in a toast to a grinning British soldier.

How do I know it was the detested alcohol, forbidden to all believers? Because of the label: the brand-name on the bottle was as carefully positioned as in an advertisement. It obscured part of a page of the illuminated Holy Koran which the ancient had no doubt been perusing when the kindly Tommie invited him to a drink.

When the potential of holy war — or, at least, armed uprisings

170

— was pointed out to the (British) Middle East experts who were behind all this, it must be admitted, to their credit, they flapped quite a bit. Luckily, in another triumph for Muddling Through, news soon came that the whole consignment of posters had been dive-bombed and sunk in a Malta convoy by the *Luftwaffe*.

Of course that was years and years ago. The tradition is, however, upheld by those like the BBC radio reporter who ended an interview with the President of the Council for Mosques by telling the devout Muslim: 'I expect now you could do with a drink'.

Some people might conclude that the Middle East advisers were useless, and that they should have got the sack immediately. But, (though I can't explain the BBC man's words) after reading an autobiography of an experienced British traveller, I have realised that actions like offering pigs' meat to Muslims springs from delicacy rather than the reverse. Major-General Sir Thomas Fraser (KCB CMG PSC REI) made it clear as far back as 1914 that foreigners cannot be understood.

> 'One must keep in mind,' he says, 'that no foreigner can truly gauge the methods of another race, and least of all can Europeans do so in the case of Asiatics.'[2]

Perhaps the Egyptians do not count as Asiatics, or perhaps exceptions prove the rule, but there is one case at least where an Englishman fell foul of another Englishman and managed to get out of trouble through an Egyptian.

Colonel André von Dumreicher relates that, while on official duty in the desert at Matruh:

> I received a wire from the Ministry that a British officer — Captain Douglas — had pulled the Debba station-master's ear, and had threatened him with a revolver. The station-master had complained to the Khedive — the owner of the railway — and His Highness had sent his master of ceremonies to Lord Kitchener, who ordered a strict enquiry to be made. Douglas, quite unaware of the seriousness of his offence, which nearly led to his dismissal, reported that he had arrived at Debba after I had left. Hearing that there was going to be a fight at the rail-head against 600 bedouins he had wanted to join me at once. The station-master, a Nationalist, refused

to give him a special train. Douglas then seized the man by the ear, calling him a few choice names, and threatened him, not with a revolver, but with a small atomizer which he carried in his pocket on account of his influenza. As Douglas was really a capital fellow, I explained that he had only been in the country a few months and that the whole incident was due to his zeal and his wish to help me out of a tight corner. But Lord Kitchener remained adamant, and said that Douglas must resign. Douglas, however, showed that he was a good diplomat as well as a smart soldier . . . he had been transferred to Amaid . . . The Khedive, visiting Amaid a few weeks later, was received by Captain Douglas in charge of the guard of honour, which consisted of the whole available force, i.e., one corporal and two men . . . On the Khedive's saying that he was pleased with the troops, Douglas burst out: 'Will Your Highness please protect me against Lord Kitchener, who wants to sack me for pulling the station-master's ear at Debba. Will Your Highness ask the station-master here if I am bad?' This worthy official stepped forward with his daughter of six and his boy of eight and swore that Captain Douglas was in fact the nicest man in the world; that he had taught his children English, and that they loved him as an uncle. The Khedive, who had a great sense of humour, intervened with Lord Kitchener in Douglas's favour and he was allowed to remain in the Egyptian Government service.[3]

Of course, Douglas tends to be a Scottish name, so that might account in part for his disinclination just to muddle through.

On the other hand, Douglas spoke French and so did the Egyptian ruler, so they were in more direct communication than is usual in British-foreign interaction.

French was at the time the language of international diplomacy and politics. Indeed, one of the suggested causes of English upper-class hostility to the French is the way the 'Froggies' laughed at the Anglo-Saxons trying to speak it, from the 11th century onwards.

I recall a retired diplomat of the old Austro-Hungarian Empire reminiscing about the 'Great Old Days'. At dinner parties the length and breadth of Europe before the First World War (provided no Britisher was present) guests could be relied on to rock with laughter at the story of one British statesman's attempt to make a major speech in French. (The tale is still told of contemporary British figures, usually with the setting changed to Brussels.)

'Quand je vois ma derrière,' he is reported to have said, *'je vois que c'est dividé en deux parts'*. He meant to say, of course, 'When I review my past, I see that it is divided in two parts'.

It seems to be built into the national psychology that Brits abroad are expected to look after themselves rather than appeal to other Britons for help. Those who apply to the consulates and embassies overseas often experience this at first hand. The papers scream about it – naturally to no avail.

John Carne, writing in the nineteenth century, proves that the tradition of self-sufficiency is longstanding. Sailing from Constantinople for Ismir, then known as Smyrna, he recalls:

> It was a lovely moonlight night when we lost sight of the Dardanelles; and a fine wind bore us towards Scio. On board were two natives of the northern part of England, who had gone to Persia with the hope of getting rich by engaging in a cotton-manufactury, set up at Tebriz by a young English merchant. The latter had lost all his little property in the attempt, having been deluded, he said, by false representations; and, at last, after a long and difficult journey over-land with the two natives of Lancashire, had succeeded in reaching Constantinople. To hear the latter, in their broad provincial dialect, relate their adventures in Persia – their passage over mountains covered with snow and plains parched with heat, half starved at one time, and abused or pursued at another – was very amusing.[4]

Of course, not all British people have travelled abroad to admire the scenery or to provide entertainment for their compatriots. You may recall that Charles M. Doughty, the celebrated explorer, describes one Englishman's harmonisation with his surroundings, in his *Wanderings in Arabia*[5]. As usual, the tale is told in the quasi-biblical English that appears to be Mr. Doughty's own attempt at harmonising:

> One day Aman [a Jeddah customs officer] watched upon a

steamship newly arrived from India, and among her passengers was a 'Nasrany' [Nazarene/Westerner] who sat 'weeping — weeping and his friends could not appease him.'

Aman, when he saw his time, enquired the cause; and the stranger answered him afflictedly, 'Eigh me! I have asked of the Lord that I might visit the City of His Holy House, and become a Moslem: is not Mecca yonder? Help me, thou good Moslem, that I may repair thither, and pray in the sacred places! But ah! These detain me.'

When it was dark, Aman hired a wherry; and privily he sent this stranger to land, and charged the boatman for him.

The Jidda waterman set his fare on shore; and saw him mounted upon an ass for Mecca; one of those which are driven at a run, in a night-time, the four and forty miles or more betwixt the port town and the Holy City.

When the new day was dawning, the 'Frengy' [Frank] entered Mecca! Some citizens, the first he met, looking earnestly upon the stranger, stayed to ask him, 'Sir, what brings thee hither — being, it seems, a Nasrany!'

He answered them, 'I was a Christian, and I have required it of the Lord, that I might enter this Holy City and become a Moslem!'

Then they led him, with joy, to their houses, and circumcised the man: and that renegade or traveller was years after dwelling in Mecca, and in Medina. Aman thought his godfathers had made a collection for him; and that he was become a tradesman in the suk.

Of course, as the admirable adage has it, circumstances alter cases, and we must look at a whole range (currently fashionable English phrase) of experiences to see the British track-record in living and travelling abroad.

Colonel H. R. P. Dickson seems to have belonged to the harmonisation school. Spending a lot of time with bedouins, who pray five times a day, he naturally was often with them during their devotions. He tells us:

> The sight is a simple and inspiring one, and I for one always remove my European head-dress when in the presence of the Badawi at prayer.[6]

Colonel Dickson spent many decades among these fierce fellows without ever guessing something which a Muslim would have known since his earliest years: it is a discourtesy to take off your hat in the East. To do so just before or during prayers is even worse; and may even be seen as an insult.

So perhaps the fact was that the Bedouins were treating him like a guest. Therefore, they had for umpteen years overlooked what would have seemed to them a solecism akin to − or perhaps even worse than − telling an Englishman that he had no sense of humour, or was a bad driver, or even that he looked like a proper Charlie.

If we have been concentrating rather much upon the Middle East, this may be because the British are obsessed by it at the moment. They have what is called 'a residual interest' (sometimes, even, depending upon which specialist you are reading, 'a continuing moral responsibility') in the area.

It used, of course, to be called 'an imperial responsibility', or 'strategic lifelines'; but it all means the same thing, which you are invited to interpret for yourself. After all, this *is* a handbook, and should have some exercises and difficult bits, to keep the reader fresh.

Edging away from the East, we discover that some British people are keen to know as much as possible about the people and places which they visit. Others, however, consider curiosity as something inelegant. 'The Athenians,' writes Charles Graves, brother of the poet Robert,

> 'stare more unashamedly than people anywhere else in the world. They stare at your face, your clothes, your shoes. The only thing to do is to stare back.'[7]

It was Charles who said to me once: 'Robert and I are half-German and half-Irish, which means that we are experts on the English, which is better than actually *being* English'. So here you have the definitive English response to Athenians.

Of course, if you are English, you will wish to avoid people thinking that you are looking too much at too many things. There is obviously an art in this. The Victorian traveller J.J. Aubertin remarks:

'I think it is a great mistake to be making a point of gaping at everything. It spoils the eye and confuses the memory, and emanates from mere childish curiosity to see, and to be able to answer "Did you see?" It is sometimes a luxury to be able to say "No".'[8]

And there is such a thing as wasting words, even in a travel book. Mr. Aubertin gives us an example of dealing with foreign sights and people, which he tidies up with an interesting economy of phrase, quite devoid of any 'childish curiosity':

What I soon noticed was that the Burmese are very fond of colour. Palm trees, tamarind trees, and mango trees mingled their various foliages. It would be difficult to describe the city [Rangoon] farther, because there is nothing to describe.

Mr. Aubertin reminds me of a certain colonel, in J.H. Rivett-Carnac's *Many Memories,* where a wonderful lesson in dealing with the people of the Far East is given:

It is related how a young ensign, who had been brought up at an Indian hill-school and had only passed a couple of years in Europe before obtaining his commission, presented himself for examination. Having spoken Hindustani all his life, he did not regard the simple colloquial test with any great anxiety. At the close of the day the secretary of the committee said: 'Of course we pass Ensign W—-; he speaks the language like a native'. 'Exactly,' growled the old Colonel, the President; 'he speaks the language like a *native*, but he don't speak it like a *gentleman*, and I won't pass any officer who don't speak the language like a gentleman.'[9]

I wonder whether the Colonel could have been the same officer who is said to have met a tragic end during the Second World War because he spoke Hindustani like a gentleman. The story concerns a General (he would have been a colonel at about the right time) who was addressing a parade of Indian Muslim *Sowars*, cavalrymen, on a morale-boosting tour.

All morning, the purple-faced, be-medalled old codger had been poking around the military base: for was he not himself an old cavalryman? He was escorted by a young Indian officer (the thin end of the wedge was even then apparent) who kept on suggesting that the General might perhaps like to speak to the men in English, which they all understood well.

'Nonsense!' roared the old man; 'do them a world of good to hear me in my Hindustani: motivate them, know what I mean?'

The difficulty was that the old gent, like all his kind, had cloth ears, and pronounced *Sowar*, cavalryman, as *Suwar*, which means swine.

The General outranked everyone else on parade, so the other officers shrugged helplessly as he stepped onto the podium.

'I am a *Suwar*!' he announced. British officers, especially high-ranking ones, were so often reputed to be drunk, that the *Sowars* merely stiffened.

'And,' continued the ancient warrior, 'I am the son of a *Suwar*!'

Still discipline held.

Until the General ended triumphantly with: 'And you, too, are all *Suwars* − and sons of *Suwars*!'

Lances at the ready − as it is still related in officers' messes across India, Pakistan and Bangladesh − they charged him. The official explanation was: 'this gallant officer, answering the call of duty, died of heat-stroke on the parade ground, while exhorting the troops.'

Newspaper correspondents in India, as others elsewhere today, like to pepper their reports with local words, to give the impression that they speak the language like natives. One London war correspondent must surely have asked a few barmen for phrases, and tipped insufficiently. The real translation of the words in his report is in square brackets:

> The brave Gurkhas charge into battle waving their *Chilumchis* [enamel bowls] or swords, and crying *"Suwar ka bacha!"* [son of a swine!] or God Be with Us . . .

Forty, eighty or ninety years ago, if you did not behave as a British onlooker expected, you were a proper target for criticism. Why, if you weren't conducting yourself like a gentleman, you might − Heaven forbid − find yourself likened to such things as, say, a French waiter. So have things changed?

Up to a point, perhaps. But when the erstwhile French President Mitterand attended the Japanese Emperor's funeral, *The Independent Magazine* gleefully reported his was:

by far the deepest bow . . . rather, I note, like a French waiter presenting a large bill — and, indeed, he is reported to have had lengthy talks with the Japanese Finance Minister only the day before the funeral.[10]

So, be warned, in case you look like a French President sometime.

The British have another priceless asset in dealing with foreigners. You don't have to go Abroad to note how funny, ridiculous or unacceptably different it is. You can satisfy yourself as to its peculiarities or unacceptability from the comfort of your own easy chair at home. Of course, the British always prefer to use humour as a weapon, especially where people suspected of being in any way Germanic are involved.

Thus it was that a court case in Frankfurt, Germany, made the front page of one British serious national daily, and appeared in London's evening newspaper the same day. Even though the story had no link with Britain it was told with plenty of relish. It concerned a Caribbean cruise which became a nightmare for a couple who found

> 500 of the 600 fellow passengers were members of the Swiss Union of the Friends of Folk music, who were not only in full voice but had with them a variety of musical instruments. The 500 were keen on doing the kind of things members of the Swiss Union of the Friends of Folk Music like to do.
>
> Groups such as the Lisbeth Sidler-Fritz Arnet Yodelling Duet and the Village Sparrows of Oberéageri serenaded all passengers, including the less than enthusiastic. The Swiss brass band drowned out even the sounds of the Latin American midnight buffet promised in the brochure, the court was told.[11]

It is almost as if the British Press found satisfactory the news that both lots of foreigners got their come-uppance: the Germans were infuriated and the Swiss were less than appreciated — the tour company was ordered to pay 30% compensation. In his beautifully-written piece in the Independent, Steve Crawshaw remarks:

> Now welcome to a new concept: discounts for holidays with too much yodelling.

This innovative departure comes to you courtesy of the Frankfurt District Court which . . . decreed that an excess of alpenhorns, yodelling and similar music-making is a legitimate reason for holidaymakers to demand their money back . . .

The court took a dim view of the mental torture and argued that the possibility of non-stop Swiss folk music was not something a holidaymaker planning to float around the Caribbean could reasonably expect.

Being rude about people is an almost-perfected art. And, of course, if anyone else is rude about you, or even annoys you, strike back as soon and as hard as possible.

I have not heard of any Swiss being rude about the British, but I can offer one about the Americans, just as a paradigm, this time from Peter McKay. It could probably be adapted for Swiss brass bands, Indian curries or Patagonian turkey:

> We have come to a pretty pass when Americans call us vulgar. No nation on earth has equalled the American talent for vulgarity.
>
> Famous Americans live on the same cultural level as British time-share tycoons. Americans have made a virtue of vulgarity. It is their plucky way of fashioning an alternative to Europe's inimitable style.[12]

There's always *something* unacceptable to point out about Abroad and its people. For instance, if Salvador Dali can be dismissed as 'a greasy foreign painter'[13], who would want to have much to do with anybody Abroad?

A British Ambassador in Europe is quoted by Sir Roy Denman (who was until 1989 Head of the Delegation of the Commission of the EC, in Washington), as denouncing both British membership and the Community itself:

'Her Majesty's government,' thundered His Excellency, 'could never associate with that Continental ragtag and bobtail − but it was damned impertinent of them to think of going it on their own!' He spoke for a British attitude.

21

Loathsome or Lovable?

> Have the English become an unpleasant race?
> The Archbishop of Canterbury, Dr. George
> Carey, thinks so, and one imagines Her
> Majesty, if she were free to speak, would say
> so, too. Everybody is saying so ...
> Mr. Auberon Waugh . . . claims we are not
> merely unpleasant, but extraordinarily so –
> 'mean, envious, full of rancour, hatred and
> bogus self-righteousness.'
>
> – *The Evening Standard*[1]

The above quotation is from a full-page article by Stanley
Reynolds, illustrated by a repellent picture of what can only be
called a very criminal-looking John Bull, in bovver-boots with
apelike jaw. It is entitled:

WHY HAVE WE BRITISH BECOME SO LOATHSOME?

The author says that the greed, taste for mockery and fast-
developing pride of the British

> will continue to continue [*sic*] until it becomes so bad that
> the Archbishop of Canterbury and Mr. Waugh and Her
> Majesty the Queen will have to find some other country to
> pray, write and reign in while we remain and go, not quietly,
> mad.

Thus an Englishman on his fellow-countrymen.

Loathsome or lovable, the British are usually viewed by people
of many different nationalities with wonderment. Sometimes this
is conditioned by their experiences, and can be highly subjective.

There is an Arabian proverb, current among those who have

pretensions to gentility, which says that 'Even one day's goat-herding may make a boor of you'. I have spent a lot of time among the British. The effect of this saying, if true, may have coloured my opinion of them. I do not find them loathsome at all. In fact, I find myself infuriating other foreigners by my British habits: which they often regard as loathsome.

In particular, people all over the world are complaining more and more about the British practice of behaving or talking indirectly. It takes this form: *Not* 'Could you post this letter for me?' *But* 'Are you passing that pillar-box at the end of the street on your way into Town?' *Not* 'Can you meet me at 6 tomorrow?' *But* 'Are you doing anything at about six tomorrow?' *Not* 'Have you seen my hat?' *But* 'You know that hat of mine?'

It's one of those mannerisms that really drive people crazy. I've heard foreigners say: 'If another Englishman says to me "You know that train that starts from the *Gare du Nord*?" — I shall go stark, staring mad . . .'

I was quizzing an old Indian servant about the behaviour of the English, when he said, 'Ask me for incidents, Sahib: they always used to show us what the *Angrezis* (English) were like during the British Raj, though of course we sometimes did not know what they meant.'

I asked him to give me an instance of British indirectness, which he had said he found the most baffling characteristic.

'My old Sahib and his Memsahib always had a boiled egg each for breakfast. Every day they had it, for the twenty years I was with them they never missed a day or an egg.

'One night he was taken ill, and called for me in his fever. I realised he was on his death bed only because he said, when I came near, "Ram Lal, it will be just the one egg tomorrow for breakfast — for the Memsahib only!"'

So, for all those people of English background: this too could be used as a way of dealing with foreigners. Drive them crazy with the indirect approach.

I asked a French family in Biarritz if they had anything to contribute to the debate. Naturally I approached it this way: 'You know the English?' 'Yes'. 'You know that they are famous for dealing with foreigners?' 'Ye—es' — and so on, until I got to:

'What experience have you of the English when they're dealing with foreigners?'

When they had stopped laughing, crying, biting their nails and so on, the paterfamilias told me their story.

They were reasonably devout, in the manner of French people, and one Christmas they had an English gentleman as a house guest. They thought it might be pleasant, and also an introduction to higher Catholic things, if they took him to midnight Mass.

Walking home after the service, they fell to discussing it in their usual manner. The grandmother thought that there might have been more candles; the mother that the bells pealed a little too loudly for her nerves; the daughters found the incense wearisome; and the son of the house, naturally being something of an intellectual, spoke about the content of the sermon.

The Englishman, their guest, whose presence had been temporarily forgotten in the exchange of ideas, suddenly stopped and stabbed the ferrule of his umbrella into the cobbles.

'Well,' he drawled, 'you may say what you like, but *I* say it was a damned good show for a penny.'

My French friends are still not sure who was dealing the more effectively with whom. He was, and remains, a mysterious foreigner to them. They were, and are, foreigners to him. He dealt with them all right: but perhaps without realising that he was doing so. This sort of behaviour may, indeed, be the origin of the British assertion: 'We always treat foreigners exactly as we treat one another.'

The son of the house (who possesses I don't know how many quarterings to his shield and a good Sorbonne philosophy degree) has constructed several theories about all this. Since, however, he is also good at karate and fencing, and will probably read this book, I think I'll quit while I'm ahead where this story is concerned.

Is the British person likeable or loathsome? The soppier British occasionally publish sentimental pieces claiming to be the former because of their kind hearts, democracy, love of dogs and so on; and fear that they are the latter because of their bovver-boys.

Perhaps, without offence, I might try to broaden the canvas. I believe that things are not reducible to a binary mode as the tabloid Press insists. And a lot depends on what you choose as your criteria. Arabs, for instance, may mean sand and palm-trees, or even worse, to the British. What are the Brits to the Arabs, I wondered ... So I asked a Gulf Sheikh whom I know well, and whom I knew would answer me without regard to the answer he thought I wanted.

It was well worth it.

'I love them,' he said, and explained why.

'There were two Englishmen here at a bloodstock sale. And you know how they like horses, though we have some thousands of years start on them here, as it were.

'Well, they bought one each, took them back to their hotel and tethered them on a patch of lawn there. So as to make sure that each would recognise his own horse in the morning, they tied a coloured headcloth on the mane of one steed, and went to bed.

'In the morning, the two went out to look at their horses. Unfortunately, the headcloth had come loose, and was lying on the ground. How were they to know which mount was which? They puzzled and puzzled, and for some time could not think of a way to tell one horse from the other.

'"I tell you what" said one Englishman to his fellow, "we'll just choose one each − there are, after all, only two, and they cost us about the same. You take first pick."'

'"Right," said his friend, "sounds fair enough. This time I'll have the white horse and you have the black!"'

'Yes − I really love them! They love horses, you see,' said my Arabian friend.

This, of course, seems to be a story along the lines of those about Westerners buying any old caviar in Russia, or Americans intoxicated with cashmere twinsets in London; and (perhaps especially) Arabs drinking from finger-bowls at Buckingham Palace.

There is, perhaps, rather more edge to the story from the alleged reminiscences of a Japanese magnate who was recruiting senior executive staff in London, for his British operation. I was told the tale by a Far Eastern ambassador with whom I was discussing the developing economies of the Pacific Rim countries. It concerns the recruiting agent of a Japanese tycoon who was interviewing a candidate for the post of London sales director for his company.

'Mr. Jones, you have been in charge of sales for a major

British concern. How would you describe your skills?'

'Well, I do a lot of fishing and shooting, play roulette quite a bit, and ride to hounds three times a week.'

'Anything else?'

'Yes. I go to Ascot, Henley and Glyndebourne.'

'And?'

'And I dictate letters to my secretary in the back of the Rolls-Royce on the way to Wimbledon, Wembley Stadium or business-lunches, that kind of thing.'

The Japanese reported: 'I simply had to tell the gentleman, "I am so sorry, but you are over-qualified."'

Of course, neither man may have been typical enough for us to learn from him how to deal with foreigners; but I wonder whether the Japanese gentleman was being candid or diplomatic when he gave his answer. Like many good ambassadorial tales, this one was left hanging just where I have ended it.

That Englishman sounded very like the one whom I overheard confusing a foreign companion when the pair were sitting beside me on the top deck of a London tourist bus. The Englishman was reading out signboards above shops. Suddenly, his voice took on a strange note.

'GENTLEMEN'S OUTFITTERS!' he rumbled. 'Damned contradiction in terms. Gentlemen are never *outfitted*, except for Africa and so on, and then only with mosquito nets and the rest. Gentlemen have tailors.'

Certainly of the same school was the individual who, according to Mallorcan folklore, arrived on the island with Rolls and chauffeur and after a fairly short visit instructed: 'Smithson, I'm tired of life. Just drive us over that cliff, will you?'

Some of these situations are more difficult than they seem. When I told this story to an English lady, she only said, 'Mallorca as bad as that, eh?'

In Mallorca, the old-time English foreigner has made an abiding impression. His or her way of dealing with the Mallorquins caused a reaction which persists: a mixture of affection and puzzlement, quite unsusceptible to the kind of — shall I call it robust? — analysis we get almost daily in the British Press, offering us the sole options of Loathsome or Lovable.

22

Can Foreigners Deal with the British?

Pablo: 'What a beautiful day this is ...'

Pedro: 'Yes, but look at all the English having it, too ...'

— Joke current in Marbella

The short answer to the question contained in the title of this chapter is, I suppose, No.

Or, at least, Not Without Difficulty. Foreign comments on the British tend to be adulatory or hostile. Humour is seldom to be seen. However, myriad works about the Sceptred Isle and its denizens continue to appear all over the world, especially in Europe.

Some are borderline. I am not sure, for instance, whether this is funny or just competitive. It was told to me by a seafaring Maltese-American:

Q: Why are British naval officers so snooty?
A: Well, we join the Navy to see the world. The Brits join it for the world to see them.

When allied servicemen visited Turkey during the Gulf War, Turkish liaison officers 'had nothing but praise' for the Yanks on shore-leave from visiting warships. But the British sailors were another matter. Talking about the men from HMS *Penelope*, in port at Antalya at the same time, a Turkish soldier seemed confused. 'What's the matter with them?' he asked; 'I never saw people before who just want to drink themselves to oblivion'.[1]

I expect that if I were English, I'd have enough *nous* to be able to say that this incident disproves the aspersions in the Maltese-

American joke. British tars are accused of being snooty when they are just drunk.

A lot of frustration is due, I am sure, to the foreigner not knowing how to get a rise out of an Englishman. You can almost feel the near-desperation of D.W. Brogan[2] (in *The English People*) when he reports that the British have, 'at one end of Whitehall a statue of Charles I and at the other a statue to Cromwell who cut off Charles's head.'

Brogan cites this fact to indicate how little the British could understand the enmities of Europe. His book seems to me to demonstrate just as strongly how little the foreigner might be able to deal with the British.

Of course, as the country becomes more multi-cultural, it is sometimes hard to tell *who* the British actually are. When I am talking to people about the British these days, I'm often told, almost with indignation: 'But *you are* British!'

Last time I was in Spain cashing a traveller's cheque, the bank teller pointed to the queue at a nearby window and said, 'Please explain one thing to me.'

'Something wrong with the cheque?'

'No, of course not. But how is it that all these people from Asia and Africa have British passports?'

I could only refer him to a news item I carry in my wallet and let him work out the rest (it is from *Holme Valley Express*, a respected English local newspaper).

> An Upperthong family spent New Year's Eve over 1,700 miles apart when the issue of a visa went disastrously wrong. But Slaithwaite-based Travelworld claim they did not realise Mr. Khosraw Asghari-Ziba was not English.

I am not sure whether you could put the changing nature of Englishness down to foreigners successfully dealing with the British. But there is an enormous wealth of stories in the East — far more than in Europe or America — of contact, conflict and coexistence of the Brits with the local people.

It must be admitted that the Anglo-Saxon, and even the Celt, is more at home when operating on his islands than in some hot and dusty place where he may even have to take off his shoes and keep on his hat in the house. Or where, having politely admired something, he is tiresomely forced to accept it as a gift.

Again, the reader may decide who came out best in this famous tale of the Gulf:

In the first few years of the twentieth century, there was a British Political Agent responsible for what was regarded as the Protectorate of Kuwait: a quite common situation on the peripheries of the Empire.

This Agent was a certain Captain Shakespeare. Not only was he disliked for his activities – meddling, it was called – among the people of the Sheikh's domains, but he did not manage to establish good personal relations with local notables because of his youth and inexperience.

Indeed, he and Sheikh Mubarak were, after a time, almost at daggers drawn. Sheikh Ahmad ibn Jabir told my father: 'My grandfather couldn't decide if the English King had sent Shakespeare to us as an insult: perhaps because of some imagined slight; or whether he really did not have anyone better under his command.'

Captain Shakespeare's supplies used to arrive in Kuwait by mailboat. It was the gallant Captain's custom to race out to where it was riding at anchor, to place his own boat alongside, seeking to board her before anyone else and insisting on being first to claim his mail and supplies.

He felt that he had to do this because, in spite of his constant applications, he had not been officially recognised as having any prior right to primacy in getting onto the ship. He felt he needed it as His Britannic Majesty's representative.

Sometimes he got to the mailboat first, sometimes not. To the Kuwaiti boatmen who also rushed for the mailboat, this was normal behaviour for bumboat men: but certainly not for someone with Shakespeare's pretensions.

They saw him as some sort of eccentric with delusions of importance. This, of course, he did not know, as he never troubled himself to enquire about local customs or opinions, but tried to impose his own, which were seldom, if ever, locally regarded as superior.

On the occasions when the Captain managed to reach the mailboat first, he had to jump aboard very smartly, since there was always a crowd of Kuwaiti boats in hot pursuit: and a moment lost might rob him of his coveted place.

One day he just managed to go alongside ahead of several other boats; but, before he could tie his rope to the mailship, several Kuwaitis — just behind and using his craft as a stepping-stone — swarmed past him, one or two gaining the mailboat's deck first.

The Political Agent was absolutely furious. Reacting without thinking, he started to push and pull at the invading Kuwaitis, crying petulantly, 'I was here first!'

There was a roar of laughter at this, from the entire attendance of bumboaters, which only made matters worse. The Captain, now purple in the face, heaved at the Kuwaiti nearest him: and the man, losing his balance, fell to the sea.

There was a sudden hush, as everyone saw that the unfortunate fellow lay inert on the anchor.

Shakespeare climbed onto the deck of the mailboat in a state of shock. He was now comforted by a Customs officer who promised to help him solve the matter of this unfortunate death.

The Captain, trembling in every limb, was taken straight to the Emir's Court, where the two men lined up to wait, in Arab fashion, for the judgment of the Ruler.

When their turn came, Shakespeare confessed what had happened, expressing his deep regret and offering to pay compensation to the dead man's relatives.

When he had finished, standing miserably with head hung, and the witness had had his say, the Emir burst out laughing. He said:

> 'My child, if it takes the killing of one of my people to bring you to this state of contrition and maturity, and to quieten your arrogance, then you have my permission to kill someone in this manner every day; so that you may be sufficiently improved as to lead a normal human life. If the disease disappears through the use of such a medicine, take it as often as necessary: so that we may be able to enjoy friendship and proper behaviour together!'

Shakespeare paid the compensation, he and the Sheikh became friends, and a new story was born in a land of story-tellers.

The version which the *Mudir al Jumruk*, the Head of Customs, Abdul-Latif ibn Abdul-Jalil, told was a little more elaborate. He ended:

'I rewarded the Customs officer who had overseen the matter, and allowed the stevedore who had pretended to be dead to keep the compensation-money from the Captain for his trouble. He used it to entertain all the other boatmen to a great feast. Captain Shakespeare behaved after that: but I reckoned he'd better be kept in the dark about how his lesson was contrived. And he had paid for it in cash.'

Even today there are many businessmen and even diplomats in the Middle East who do not realise that, if you do a menial task, you are regarded as being of low rank. I have myself seen the managing director of a major and very respectable British firm unable to get an audience with an Eastern grandee after having been seen buying his own stamps at the local Post Office.

A member of the British diplomatic staff in one capital wondered why he was no longer receiving invitations to Royal levees. I determined, on his behalf, what the solecism had been which led to his exclusion from high society. As nobody wanted to be discourteous to his Ambassador by telling him the reason, I had to use indirect enquiries. It turned out that the unfortunate Counsellor had been spotted booking his own seat at a railway station. 'But it was first class,' he yelped, missing the point.

Money, as well as behaviour, does talk in the Gulf region: perhaps now even more than ever. No sooner was the war against Saddam Hussein over than many Kuwaitis were claiming that they had hired the foreign forces involved — British, Americans and all — as mercenaries.

According to the British National Audit Office 'Britain made more than six hundred and fifty million pounds profit on the Gulf War because contributions from foreign governments exceeded Ministry of Defence spending.'[3]

British institutions, especially educational ones, are said to be increasingly amenable to suggestions for donations and sponsorships from unlikely sources. However, I'm still not sure of the provenance of one persistent tale, which was told at High Table in an ancient university. Apparently one of England's oldest public (i.e. posh and private) schools wanted some extra cash. An American billionaire, hearing about this, and having his own priorities, invaded the Head's study.

'Here's a cheque for $50 million, which you can have if you teach my boy to speak perfect English within three months.'

'I think we can manage that,' said the delighted master.

After ninety days touring the sights of Europe, the American was back. 'Well, what do you think of my boy?'

'Well,' says the Head, 'I'll be goldurned if he ain't the smartest guy on campus.'

'Great, Dean!' says the American, and makes out a further cheque for $50 million, which he places on the Head's desk. 'That's just to show my appreciation.'

He rushed out, and the Head said to his secretary, 'I think that that covered the matter reasonably satisfactorily, Miss Jones ...'

He and Miss J. continued to congratulate themselves on their handling of the transatlantic hick. He, meanwhile, was on the telephone to a friend in Texas. 'Say, Hiram: you know that bet of ours? Right! Well, you owe me the $250 million. I've cleared a cool $150 million, after expenses. That British teacher guy's talking perfect American now ...'

23

Life In Britain

Our people are warm, generous and immensely
talented. Our countryside is bountiful and
beautiful. Our cities are being steadily restored
to glory.

                – Charles Cowley[1]

That's more like it. I had to plough through acres of gloomy
newsprint before I could find someone who seemed to think that
Britain was any good at all.

The favourite British pastime seems to be what the Brits
themselves call whingeing, mostly about their own country. But
something else strikes a visitor more than the alleged deterioration
of the place and even of the people. It is the strangeness of it
all, often subsumed, fondly but not really accurately, under the
rubric of eccentricity.

Of all peculiar things here, opinion polls seem the most
misleading. Year after year, they predict election results which
are contradicted by the event.

This could, of course, be due to the supposed British
deceitfulness – increasingly emphasised by writers – which
causes people to lie to everyone, including pollsters. Or it could
be due to the feeling (that I, as a resident here, certainly share)
that pollsters should mind their own business instead of being
paid to pester other people. Especially when they get things wrong
so often.

Dr. Robert East, of Kingston University Business School,
analysed answers to 1,100 questionnaires. He was surprised to
learn that 'Britain's shoppers "don't mind queuing"'. But are
these not the same people who rush for buses on Cricklewood
Broadway, elbowing or handbagging me aside even if I've been

there first, and have waited for half an hour in the driving rain? They cannot have developed this custom recently, for the same report discovered that shoppers had 'fixed habits'.

Of course the aspect of the matter which hits me directly is of no real moment when seen against the canvas of greater events. The last time I was out shopping I met a neighbour, a retired colonel, and spoke to him about the subject when we had eventually battled our way aboard a bus.

The old gentleman saw it from a very different point of view to that of a selfish foreigner. This is how he put it:

It's a matter of duty, this habit of sticking to habits. Makes for discipline and obedience when needed, such as in war. I can illustrate.

There was once a British District Commissioner in Africa, who received a secret signal in 1939 to this effect: WAR DECLARED STOP PLEASE ARREST ALL ENEMY ALIENS IN YOUR DISTRICT STOP.

Naturally, he went ahead, obeying orders as far as he could. His reply, sent a few days later, read: HAVE ARRESTED SEVEN DANES FIVE ITALIANS EIGHT FRENCH AND THREE AMERICANS STOP PLEASE ADVISE ME WITH WHOM WE ARE AT WAR.

The Colonel concluded, 'D'ye see what I mean? Made of the right stuff. No pussyfooting around for a man like that. Besides, I always use me tin leg to help me get on buses. Can give a queue jumper a nasty bruise.'

If you are a fellow-foreigner, take some comfort from the words of the eminent British writer and traveller Colin Thubron, quoted in *The Observer*:

> The important thing is a recognition of your own oddness. You begin to see that we, a tiny nation with quite distinct and fairly peculiar characteristics, are not the norm. You realise that you are the strange one, not the other way round.

A foreigner may be surprised that the sentiment in the quotation above is not considered too obvious to publish. Peculiar characteristics? To the outsider, life in Britain resembles a sometimes charming, but almost always eccentric looking-glass world. Even when things seem normal, you don't have to probe very far to realise that they are deeply weird.

Opening my newspapers at random, there are reports of a vicar who has locked parishioners out of a church during a row. A second newspaper has a thoughtful advertising offer for a yurt (a sort of tent which is described as 'A 3000-year-old design for desert living'). Who in Britain today might possibly need a yurt? Could it be the unfortunate parishioners, perhaps?

Then there is that most ordinary of institutions — the nice British cuppa. It is drunk here by the gallon, regardless of taste or strength (although strong is preferred). I've heard patrons of a local jumble sale remark approvingly: 'This tea is just exactly right — the colour and taste of brown paper'. Surely a cunning strategy to repel foreigners, most of whom seem to drink coffee.

How much more daunting is tea when, as often is the case, it is accompanied by a currant bun. I have been unable to discover the date from which the English started to make these buns; so it is quite possible that they have not yet perfected the art.

This could be true in the case of a relative of the bun, the scone, which may have originated in Scotland — though the word is (*Chamber's*) 'perhaps Dutch'. To further confound the foreigner, the English pronounce the word 'skone', instead of the correct Scottish rendition: 'skonn'.

The food critic, Mr. Egon Ronay was moved to criticise the scone, as evidenced in a *Times* fourth leader (kindly sent to me by Nicholas Fry Esq.):

> Mr. Egon Ronay, in a survey of tea-rooms, has been appalled by the quality of the scones served there. Many of them, he reports, were 'dehydrated, tasteless, hard and brittle', and some were so bad that they 'could have been bounced off the wall'.[2]

The writer Anthony Burgess had typically quixotic British views on food in an inteview from his Monaco home with *The Daily Mail* Saturday magazine.[3]

'I don't have lunch really,' the eminent novelist said; adding 'The only good food in the world is in Manchester. The French think their food's good, but of course it's not.'

The French, of course, are not ones to take that kind of slur lying down. Ms. Anne Elizabeth Moutet of *Le Journal du Dimanche* of Paris lets the English have it:

> It is only in England that squalid canteens called *School Dinners* could make a fortune serving boiled cabbage to City businessmen who are delighted because the waitresses give them a public spanking if they eat with their fingers.[4]

This spanking thing cannot be regarded as a permanent feature of English life, since it is traceable to traumata experienced at an early age at school.

The Independent, excellent as always on educational matters, reported the abolition of corporal punishment in the state sector in an article by Simon Midgley:

> NOW ONLY RICH CHILDREN WILL BE BEATEN
> In 1669, a schoolboy presented a petition to Parliament on behalf of children seeking to abolish corporal punishment. This week, more than 300 years later, his wish will be granted and the beatings, at least for most children, will finally stop.[5]

There was, however, a catch as far as independent schools were concerned. As the reporter said, 'those from the most comfortable backgrounds will be most likely to be beaten, a reversal of the venerable adage: "It's the rich wot gets the pleasure, it's the poor wot gets the blame."'

The British school system has often proved invaluable in dealing with foreigners. *The Standard* reported that three women employed as school helpers in Buckinghamshire were ordered to learn Bengali. After they refused, they lost their jobs.

As usual, the British merely treat others as they treat themselves. *The Times* recorded that a mathematics teacher

> was ordered to apologise after correcting a parent who argued that three times nought was three.[6]

This was in Lewisham, London. A few months later an investigation by Colin Adamson showed that there was:

> a £208,000 study commissioned by Haringey [Council] to discover why pupils think the school meals service is awful. The dinner ladies could have told the council why most pupils

would rather queue at the local fish and chip shop . . . Last year, incidentally, the same Dublin company was paid another £228,000 by Haringey to tell it that the best way to tackle filthy classrooms was to sack 100 cleaners.[7]

Life in Britain may seem strange, but it goes on, nevertheless. You may have the luck to run into the sort of experience which had a Scandinavian friend of mine murmuring: 'In Sweden, such a thing would be impossible!'

RALLY FOR DEAF ENDS IN BATTLE WITH POLICE
'The fighting broke out on Sunday after a rally for about 1500 deaf mutes at Blackpool . . . Eight deaf people, including a woman, were arrested . . .'[8]

To add to the air of impenetrable mystery, nothing is called by its proper name. I belong to a club where the Morning Room is mostly used in the afternoons; you can't get coffee in the coffee-room (which is a dining-room), the Drawing-room is a library and sometimes has a bar in it. The Annexe is largely a basement, and seems sometimes to be known as The Garden Room. Similarly, the Private Rooms of the Royal Academy are not private at all, but open to everyone.

Scandinavians please note that virtually nobody in Britain called Anderson (and there must be millions of them) is the son of anyone called Anders. The same goes for Wilson, Wilkinson, Hutchinson, Robertson, and several million others.

The Scandinavian friend I mentioned, who was appalled at the antics of the deaf, was finished off by an earnest conversation he had with a man who introduced himself as Johnson Smith.

'So, you are a blacksmith?' asked my friend.

'Certainly not! I am a lawyer.'

'Then your father was a metalworker?'

'No! He was a stockbroker.'

'I understand now. Your father was called John, and you are Johnson.'

'Of course not! His name was William, if you must know.'

'Then why are you not called Williamson or Stockbrokerson?'

'Are you trying to be funny?'

'No, only to understand.'

'Well, you're not doing too well at it, are you?'

'Give me a clue how these foreign names work.'

'I'll give you a bunch of fives if you don't watch it.'

If you are English, involved in a similar conversation, note that the thing has generally gone far enough by this stage. If a foreigner is reading these words, note that Mr. Smith may not have read them, and step smartly aside: you may be mistaken for a Clever Dick. As the redoubtable Auberon Waugh put it, the rule is:

> The English do not like people to be too clever.[9]

Indeed, they seem mystified by lots of things that foreigners might feel are already known:

> the Home Office has given three Lancashire policemen a £10,000 grant to find out what makes motorists angry.[10]

When I read these words by Kevin Eason, I had to read them again to make sure I wasn't dreaming. A local policeman whom I stopped on his beat and asked for his reactions soon reassured me. He roared with laughter:

> 'It's the police who makes 'em angry, in my experience,' he said, wiping his eyes. 'Still, if the Home Office doesn't know, why shouldn't they pay to find out?'

Since Britain is a non-intellectual (some like to say, proudly, an anti-intellectual) place, and nowadays not very religious, it will not be useful for a foreigner to search such sources as the *Dictionary of National Biography* for enlightenment about the country or life therein. Speaking of this book John Clare the Education Editor of *The Telegraph* notes that the *Dictionary* is about to be revised and that:

> The purpose of the original 22 volumes ... was to present signed biographical essays recording the lives of those thought to have made important contributions to British life.[11]

All well and good, you might say. But read further:

> Many of the authors were clergymen and their subjects were often obscure or eccentric. Some, it was later found, never actually existed.

Never actually existed? An allegedly important contributor to British life? Whose life might have been written by a clergyman?

Things must have changed a lot since 1937, when the German Kurt von Stutterheim, in *Those English!* could write of:

> the deadly monotony that envelops the daily life of the ordinary Englishman.

Visitors and those catering for them may conceivably have endless fun, if a report by the Automobile Association is anything to go by.

In a survey of 500 hotels:

> The Automobile Association found that the kleptomaniacal tendencies went far beyond the purloining of a few towels and ashtrays; items taken include a full-sized stuffed black bear, a grand piano and a 20ft dance floor carpet.[12]
>
> The Longueville Hotel in Jersey had an entire crop of onions taken, and, at the 38-bed Oaklands Hotel In Norwich, a barman and barmaid were abducted in October.

Even more revealing were the items guests left behind in their rooms. Along with sets of false teeth were gold ingots, the cremated remains of a relative and, in one instance, a sack full of cobras ... One guest at the Seacrest Hotel, Southsea, went to the tourist information office because the tail end of the 1987 hurricane, which had already ripped off the hotel roof, had kept him awake.

Getting to those hotels, (even if you leave your false teeth there) or getting away (without a full-sized stuffed black bear) depends, as often as not, on road signs.

I insist that Britain has the most extraordinary signs in the world, (apart from the one in Morocco which says, in French and Arabic: TOMBOKTOU 52 DAYS) but I never knew why everyone got lost all the time, until the Transport Correspondent of *The Telegraph* enlightened me:

> Traffic signs 'are based on stagecoach routes, causing two-thirds of drivers to lose their way when venturing off familiar roads'.[13]

Stagecoaches flourished two hundred years ago, before being supplanted by the railways.

A survey by the Department of Transport found that 60% of London's road signs were incorrect or inconsistent. Some even pointed the wrong way.

I am prepared to believe that road signs, such as they are, date from hundreds of years ago: but why have they never been changed? This, to me, is another pointer to the secret life of the British, which we have often noticed in other connexions.

I had been worrying about this road sign business for years – and saying all sorts of facile things about it: like 'the Department of Transport must be staffed by idiots' – when I came across a much more telling explanation.

Anthony Sampson had plumbed the depths:

ON THE ROAD TO NOWHERE
Any psychoanalyst confronting the British nation on the couch would surely be bound to conclude that, deep down, we don't want to know where we're going. And there is one important clue to that national psychosis which any ageing Englishman will come up with: that magical time in 1940 when all the road signs were pulled up, or turned round, to make sure that the invading Germans would not know where they were.[14]

There are other major hazards throughout the country which makes it unlikely that you will ever get where you are trying to go, as Penelope Stokes noted:

The first task is to ascertain that you are, in fact, in the correct village. True British perversity has dotted the countryside with near-homonymous place names, so that the slightest terminological inexactitude can send someone miles off course.

In our part of Berkshire, we have a Benham and a Beenham.

In next-door Hampshire, there is Curdridge close to Curbridge, just to fox the aliens. If you mistake Netley for Netley Marsh ... Southampton Water lies in your way and the dry route incorporates a dozen miles of urban traffic.

The southern half of Britain boasts eight Whitchurches, seven Ashfords, and six Bourtons. I have totted up 14 Westons and 16 Uptons.[15]

No wonder foreigners are confused.

24

Alarm and Despondency

We have no faith in ourselves, and no certainty
as to whether we wish to be, or not to be, a
self-sustaining nation.

> – Bill Jamieson,
> *The Daily Telegraph* 24 January 1993

Where are we going?
> – *The Daily Telegraph* Leader
> 27 January 1993

During World War II there was a serious criminal offence in
Britain, spreading Alarm and Despondency.

The nature and manifestations of the crime were not specified,
in characteristic British fashion. It was assumed, I suppose, that
everyone would recognise it on sight. Right-thinking citizens
would denounce malefactors to the police, judges would know
what to do with them and they would be put away at least 'for
the duration.'

As the century drew to a close in Britain, however, like the
genie imprisoned by King Solomon, escaped and malevolently
roaming – what looked very much like alarm and despondency
stalked the land. People in the media almost seemed to vie with
one another in reporting instances of it.

Now and again there was a resoundingly patriotic article which
proclaimed the exact reverse. But usually it was so maladroit that
it smelt nearly as ratty as the anti-alarm-and-despondency
products of the old, wartime Ministry of Information, more
generally nicknamed the Mystery of Misinformation.

At the turn of the twenty-first century, the newspapers
abounded with examples of gloom.

When you are British these days, according to Lynne Truss

in *The Times* you are 'already aware of being inevitably second-rate'.[1]

A leader in *The Independent on Sunday* believed 'if we feel utter despair, it is because we see no new promise. All our gods have failed.'[2]

Second rate? All our gods. What gods?

The Daily Telegraph was more detailed, in a leading article:

> A mental state of pessimistic fatalism has the country in its grip. The sense of national despondency is not purely political and economic, as the Gallup poll published in *The Daily Telegraph* today makes plain, but spans almost the whole range of human experience.[3]

At that rate, almost the entire sixty million population would have been in jail for Alarm and Despondency if they had thought like that between 1939 and 1945.

Let us look at some of the more recent manifestations of the mentality, and then see if we can find a pattern.

The Archbishop of Canterbury, Dr. George Carey, thought that people 'have grown dull' because they don't concern themselves more about the homeless. He may have been right: there are more beggars, many more, on the streets of London than in those of North Africa. In the tourist centre of Agadir, there are six beggars; in London, according to police reports, many hundreds. A British sociologist, however calculates that 'on strictly proportional grounds, there should be 1,200 beggars in London before we reach a comparable stage'.

Professor Anthony King of Essex University, said that the difficulty lay in having had too large an empire for too long. He ended by stating: 'There are more beggars in London than in Shanghai'.[4]

I haven't had the opportunity to check with a sociologist what the proportion of beggars should be in Shanghai. But perhaps we should note (for 'balance', which is constantly demanded and seldom got, by and from the media) that some people say that far from having the Empire for too long, the British Empire was the shortest-lived in history.

Be that as it may – could the Church help? People don't listen to the Church, and nowadays they even question its credentials. Many of its personnel are no better than they have to be (see daily press) and though Salvation may come through a moral crusade, it doesn't seem likely.

A moral Crusade is exactly what the good Archbishop called for. His theology, it is to be hoped, may be better than his history. If he looked up what the Crusaders did (including raping, pillaging and murdering their own co-religionists en masse), and what happened to them (put to flight and uprooted from Palestine) he might look to his metaphors.

Thus the opinion of the Church. What of, say, the Law? Well, according to *The Observer*:

> A book by the former barrister John Parris indicts the top practitioners of our criminal justice system as a bunch of crawlers, incompetents and sadists . . . 'Now at last everyone's beginning to realise what a vast conspiracy against justice the British criminal [law] system is'.[5]

It used to be said — constantly repeated, in fact — that Britain at least has a stable monarchy, enshrining the values of her society, ensuring continuity. Auberon Waugh, among a host of others, had his opinion:

> The circumstances no longer exist in which a monarchy can survive in the affection and respect of the British people. We have become a second-class nation, yearning only for third-class status.[6]

What about the Press? Have they not the true interests of the nation at heart?

Up to a point. Nowhere is Alarm and Despondency so rife. *The Independent on Sunday* ran a whole page of interviews on the theme 'What embarrasses you about Britain?'[7]

One person said the rubbish piling up in the streets; another, people sleeping in the streets; a third, how badly dressed everyone is.

Some British people (including Brian May, guitarist with the rock group, *Queen*) didn't like the war against Argentina. The military historian Professor Edward Luttwak, believed that Britain might have been saved by 'losing the silly-billy Falklands'. And Claire Rayner squirmed at how 'the private health systems of the rest of the world are sneering at us'.

People have started to think the unthinkable: British sacred cows are not so holy after all. There can be better ways of doing things, and some foreigners are using them. In a thoughtful leader *The Independent* pointed this out. The editorial implicitly emphasised that almost everything in Britain needs an overhaul: it is no longer enough to believe in the wisdom of elders and betters, whether in law, government, education, commerce or whatever; and 'people are discovering' that:

> Parliament is neither representative nor sovereign . . . many of the most important decisions affecting their lives are no longer made in Westminster but in Brussels, Washington or Tokyo, the boardrooms of multinationals and the dealing rooms of banks.[8]

Above all, the loss of some cherished dreams means that one of the most illusory and yet most deeply-imprinted fallacies must be cast away. This is that in some mysterious way, superior to everyone else, the British alone need no basic document guaranteeing their rights:

> If Britain is to find methods of government and institutions for the next century, and the public trust to support them, it will have to look more seriously at the advantages of a written constitution. Tradition no longer does the job.

British people themselves seem to believe that they are neophobes. Sir Geoffrey Howe, when Foreign Secretary, said as far back as 4 March 1986 (in *The Times*) that Britain was 'woefully slow to innovate'. And all the talk of a commerce-and-industry-led recovery was not on: Many British companies 'seem to prefer living in a fool's paradise' to competing internationally.

In addition to worrying about the legacy of empire, Professor Anthony King fretted in *The Daily Telegraph*, about Britain's economic decline. As a Canadian, he feared that UK manufacturers treated their customers 'with disdain'.[9]

British and best? We have all heard a lot about this, but Dinah Hall, in *The Evening Standard*, even took that shred of comfort away:

> We are a non-visual race, a nation which thrives on bad taste.

Cheap tat is our cultural heritage and for too long we have been deprived of it . . . you should try bad taste; it's easy, unstressful and comes so naturally.[10]

The alarm and despondency went on and on. According to *The Daily Telegraph*:

Once this country's public services were the envy of the world. Now they provoke little but pity. There cannot exist a single citizen who does not have a tale to tell of shoddiness, rudeness, tardiness, dirtiness and dreadfulness.[11]

Another major *Daily Telegraph* offering maintained:

MORE BRITONS LOSE FAITH IN POLICE, LAW, EDUCATION AND THE PRESS[12]

That story appeared in 1991, quoting a Gallup survey comparing 1989 with 1990.

Less than a year and a half later – on 22 February 1993 – things had evidently got worse. *The Daily Telegraph* published the results of another Gallup poll:

NATION'S MORALE APPROACHING A CRISIS

PESSIMISM AND LOSS OF PRIDE FACE BRITAIN OF THE FUTURE

Alarm and despondency, if not everywhere, is strongly predicted. But, pleasantly enough, it has not yet caught on everywhere. Other voices, sometimes very loud ones, have been raised in celebration of Britain, the self-renewer.

The only problem was how this renewal was to take place. At the beginning of the nineties, Martin Jacques wrote a punchy, full-page article in *The Daily Mail* entitled THE POWER THAT WILL BE OURS THROUGH EUROPE. The piece is illustrated by a picture of a small Britannia with the Union Flag on her shield, entitled 'Yesterday'. A much larger one beside it, captioned 'Tomorrow' shows the lady holding a shield with the twelve stars of Europe on it. The message, it seemed, was that Britain was planning that Anglo Saxon speciality – an imperceptible conquest of their neighbours.

Less than three months later, Lord Rees-Mogg was also

thundering away in *The Independent*. His thesis was little different, though more specific:

ANGLO-NORMANS WHO COULD CONQUER EUROPE
European federalists outside Britain ought not to be deceived by the Saxon culture of our present politics. The Norman appetite for power never sleeps. Creating a European federation could provide a new society for the Normans to seek to rule; they have, after all, dominated most of Europe before. William the Conqueror was a good European in his time.[13]

The brilliance of this particular strategy was, perhaps, the willlingness to revive the Norman element in British life without a moment's fear of losing Anglo-Saxon identity.

Lord — at that time Woodrow — Wyatt, issued a ringing, Normanesque rallying-cry in *The Times:*

The loss of empire has strengthened us. We should be confident in our remarkable recuperative powers to keep us at the top. Britain's future will be as splendid as its past.[14]

My English academic historical adviser felt it necessary to remind me at this point that:

The Normans were not too keen on being English. King Richard Coeur de Lion used to swear: 'By God! Do you take me for an *Englishman*?'

He added that he hoped Norman times would be less onerous than those uncovered at Hen Domen, the first castle of Montgomery in the Welsh borders. As *The Times* reported:

The glamorous picture of medieval castle life fostered by the cinema, with jousts and wassails in knightly halls, has received some sobering correction as a result of recent excavations at one of Britain's earliest castles.[15]

Twenty-seven seasons of excavation yielded 'no finds which could dispassionately be called aristocratic', according to Mr. Philip Baker, who directed the work for more than a quarter of a century.

Only the defences were impressive . . . and the only metal

objects are nails, knives and arrowheads. There is a distinct shortage of coins, golden goblets, arms and armour, and the other appurtenances of the medieval image.

The place is practically an Iron Age village, in strong contrast to the wealth of artefacts found in Roman excavations.

So we have latter-day Normans, emerging from the mists surrounding Britain to dominate Europe and we have a future for Britain as splendid as its past (whatever that may mean).

The prophecies we constantly hear and read may or may not be fulfilled. The British record at precognition has not been unequivocally good. Some of the dire warnings of the past now read like pages from an Alarm and Despondency text book.

John Wesley thought that giving up witchcraft would be giving up the Bible.

Television, according to an editorial in the BBC journal *The Listener*, in 1936, 'won't matter in your lifetime or mine'.

Lord Haldane, the War Minister, was noted in 1906 for his prediction that 'the aeroplane will never fly'.

Not to mention the pronouncements of Lord Kelvin (President of the Royal Society, 1890-95): 'Radio has no future' and 'X-rays will prove to be a hoax'. In 1926 Professor A.W. Bickerton castigated: 'This foolish idea of shooting at the moon' and in 1933 Lord Rutherford famously dismissed nuclear power: 'Power from atoms? Moonshine!'

It may be possible to predict deliberately; but I am still convinced that the British, when they are right, arrive at the answer by a more mysterious route.

Consider the following, which might almost be viewed as a fable summing up the entire British approach:

When the Japanese electronics concern Fujitsu moved its European head office to Germany, its British managers were forced to move there as well. They hated it. But, instead of complaining, they learned Japanese and got themselves transferred to Japan, where they persuaded their employers to take over the British computer company ICL. So, of course, they were moved back to Britain.

If I hadn't read that in *The Times*,[10] I doubt if I would have believed it. You too? See what I mean?

25

Secret Meanings, Hidden Hands . . .

> The 1989 Official Secrets Act ... imposes a
> lifelong duty of confidentiality on serving and
> former members of the security and intelligence
> services. The ban also seems to apply to dead
> agents.
>
> — *The Guardian*[1]

I realised early on in my studies that a British handbook will
contain some ploys which are well known to certain readers. There
may also be quite a few which are unusual or even unique. If
this were not so, there would be no need of a handbook, much
less one which deals with dealing with foreigners.

And that was how I discovered that there are English stratagems
so baffling that they ensnare even the English themselves. And
that is even after they have been declared to be ploys.

Take, for instance, Mr. John Pierce of Ley Farm, Chirk; a
farmer who claims he is a Saxon Freeman. He says his farm lies
in a strip of land between Offa's Dyke and Wat's Dyke which
is still under the law of King Alfred, which dates back to
AD 901. This exempted the Saxons from the taxes called rates:

> Furthermore, Mr. Pierce and his son Ian, who attended court
> in the full dress of Saxon thanes, insisted that the only oath
> that would bind their consciences was the old Saxon oath,
> last sworn at Sarum in 1086. Mr. Pierce could not actually
> recite the oath, but had it all written down for production
> when necessary.[2]

There was a hitch, once the three-page oath was produced
before the magistrates. The Saxon Sword of State, not seen since
1086, was not available: and thanes had to swear on it.

206

Mr. Pierce has a formidable record of success in establishing little-known rights. So, it strikes me that the magistrates (who were described as 'bemused') might well have been encountering a new force emerging from the secret depths of Englishry. We'll no doubt hear much more of this kind of thing.

Although the English tend to limit their traditional lore to the time of the Germanic invaders, more and more signs are emerging of a prosperous pre-Saxon culture in these islands. Hence English people are again welcoming such things as the concept of the prehistoric 'Earliest Englishman', the ancient, Celtic, Britons (Queen Boadicea among them) and – even farther back – pagan rituals.

> The Burning of Bartle, which ensures good crops, may go back to the Stone Age and is carried out by English villagers in Yorkshire every August. The idea is said to date back some 11,000 years, to the Middle East. It's thought that when Christianity arrived in Britain, the ancient practice of Bartle became associated with St Bartholomew, who happens to be patron saint of the village of West Witton.

The tradition was highlighted in *The Independent* which referred to analogous rituals in such places as Peru, Germany and Asia Minor: thus, I imagine, making possible a connexion, in UK terms, between the Brits and those mystifying foreigners.

I have dealt with the putative origins of the English in far-off Central Asia, even further away than my own Afghanistan, in *The Natives are Restless*[3]. But – 11,000 years ... Anyway, this prehistoric link may help us to understand other British rituals and superstitions. We all know that the British people are riddled with them.

There are several full-blown books and encyclopaedias on the subject of broken mirrors, black cats, rabbits' feet, dreams and so on.

Of course, if the ravens leave the Tower of London, dreadful things will happen. As to the apes leaving Gibraltar: it doesn't bear thinking of. Just as well the British are such rational people, or their superstitions surely would have sunk them ages ago.

I was once refused coffee by our maid, when I asked for it. She justified her attitude by repeating: 'Tea after beef, if not, you're a thief!'

The Oxford Dictionary of English Proverbs, (1970) teems with wise sayings to guide the irrational:

> SOW PEAS AND BEANS IN THE WANE OF THE MOON;
> WHO SOWETH THEM SOONER, HE SOWETH TOO SOON.

And

> THEY THAT MARRY IN GREEN, THEIR SORROW IS SOON SEEN.

But:

> YELLOW'S FORSAKEN, AND GREEN'S FORSWORN, BUT BLUE AND RED OUGHT TO BE WORN.

This is despite the fact that since World War II, there has been a flurry of debunkery of English history and British customs. For example, about how Sir Walter Scott invented the Scotland of the Victorian images and how the Victorians conjured up all kinds of traditions and inventions about Merrie England.

Recent Brits seem to treat facts in an equally cavalier manner. The glaring errors in new history textbooks, for instance. Christopher Booker observes:

> The distinguished historian of Roman Britain Dr. Graham Webster filled eighteen pages with such errors, just from books on his own period.[4]

And, it seems, new superstitions are constantly being created. At ITV's headquarters in London, plaques were once put up all over the building. They were inscribed 'A Winning Team for '93'. To help staff participate in the gaining of a new contract, employees were encouraged to touch these as they passed.

And there is, of course, the modern cult of political correctness (PC) whose devotees show an almost superstitious aversion to anything which contradicts their imagined view of people and the world.

Nor is scientific training proof against a superstitious outlook – or even an interest in the occult.

Dr. William Sargant, the illustrious psychologist – an expert on brainwashing and conditioning and author of *Battle for the Mind*[5] — was as level-headed as anyone I have met. His books are classics, and have helped enormously in the struggle for commonsense, and against cults and indoctrination.

But, hearing that I had written a book on magic (*Oriental Magic*)[6], he bombarded me with telephone calls, asking for 'spells that would work'. He wanted to try them out. When I told him that my books on this subject were descriptive and not instructional and moreover were employed in university anthropology courses, he became quite annoyed. When I published *The Secret Lore of Magic*[7], a survey of Western magical literature, he became positively furious. I had not, it seems 'revealed whether I believed in the materials or not'.

I had to defend myself energetically to the effect that it was surely to my credit that one could not detect bias in my work, rather than the reverse. In the end, he said, 'I see what you mean. Strange that I did not spot that flaw in my reasoning. Shows you how conditioned we all are.'

Luckily, we eventually became good friends, and he lectured for me (at the Institute for Cultural Research) but it was difficult at first to shake him from his determination to discover my secrets. 'Knowledge of conditioning' as he said, 'does not protect one against it.'

Dr. Gerald Gardner, the old Malaya hand and weapons buff, who had a witchcraft museum in the Isle of Man, was convinced that I had psychic powers, and tried to get me to 'bind' an enemy of his.

Once he even lured me to his Maida Vale flat in London claiming he had a secret plan. There he 'confessed' that he had concocted the entire cult of witchcraft which he called the Wicca. It had naked 'rituals' because he was a voyeur and it had chastisement because he liked being 'gently whipped'.

Having unburdened himself of this information (which was quite unsolicited and of no interest to me) he demanded, as a *quid pro quo*, 'spells that would work'. I told him that, on the contrary, I wanted to know some of his secrets. All he would tell me was 'you have just heard them!'

The 'secret plan' included a partnership for me in the 'wicca' and in his witchcraft museum on the Isle of Man. I turned it down.

A widely respected former editor of *The Spectator*, and himself a writer of books on the supernatural, contacted me again and again, asking to be taught the 'secrets' of my Sufi cult. I told him that I had no cult and that I had written numerous books on Sufism which showed that it was *sui generis*, something of an unique kind, and not a cult at all.

At this he only became more interested by my 'novel way of concealing' the deep mysteries of the system written about in *The Sufis*[8] and *The Way of the Sufi*[9], which were supposed to be explanatory enough: and, indeed, had sufficed many people to perceive the nature of Sufi thought.

It took me years to shake him off.

Mysterious beliefs and the desire for secrets among the British are echoed by equally inexplicable happenings. Both things are presumably caused by some secret group mind or inner intention which helps the British to keep foreigners at bay, striking fear and confusion into their hearts.

It is worth reviewing a few more incidents, though I see little hope of understanding any of them. Though not overtly supernatural, who is to say what their true origin is?

For example, a Mr. Gervas Steele of Norfolk wrote a letter to the Editor of *The Times*. In it he explained that his home had been burgled and property stolen. It was kept by the police as evidence until the case was heard. After the case was over, Mr. Steele was free to take his items away. He continues:

> My car was quite inadequate for the job and there was no time at the end of the day to arrange for a carrier. I had no option but to accept the offer from the convicted burglar, who had received a suspended sentence, to drive them back for me to the house – which he did.[10]

But we should remember, when faced by seemingly impenetrable mysteries, that a great many, perhaps most, things are generally thought to be secret here. One of the first things that foreigners notice is how secretive the English are. And, I freely confess, I am so used to it that it only hits me when I have been away and return after a fairish long time.

There is just a chance that the younger generation, growing up, may be a little less secretive. One foreign undergraduate I know, struck by the impenetrability of almost everything here, told me this joke recently. It would probably have been unknown in this form twenty years ago:

> First Englishman: 'Why didn't you tell me that this horse was lame when you sold it to me?'
> Second Englishman: 'I bought it from a man who didn't mention it − so I thought it was a secret.'

And there is, after all, a great deal of fun in England, even in everyday life. An English person − or a foreigner − could have an interesting day, it appears, by emulating *The Daily Mail.* Reporters took a picture to eight auctioneers to have its price determined. The result? *'Six valued it at £150 or less ... It's worth £250,000.'* [11]

Perhaps you might be the lucky winner of a chance to take part in a *Reader's Digest* prize draw. You can even win, it seems, if you're dead. *The Daily Telegraph* records that Oscar Wilde, no less, received a letter at his address in Chelsea, informing him that: 'some people are just "born lucky" − and you could be one of them'. [12] This, despite the fact that he died in 1900.

And, in Britain, you can always get a measure of justice, whatever people may say. *The Times* Diary notes:

> Mrs. Maggie Backhouse has just divorced her husband Graham, serving a prison sentence for murdering a neighbour and trying to blow her up with a car bomb. Her grounds: unreasonable behaviour. [13]

Lord Hailsham, the former Lord Chancellor, once insisted that the English rules of evidence and procedure in the criminal courts are in a state of

> almost ludicrous artificiality, complication and want of logic that characterises our criminal code. [14]

There are so many anomalies about the law in Britain, against a repeated cry that it has the best form of justice in the world, that any foreigner is bound to conclude that there is something very odd going on.

Whatever it is, I am not at all certain that the whole story may be explained in terms of bad law or crazy judges, as some in the media seem to think. There are deeper conundrums.

Take British Telecom, the telephone and communications company. After a British national newspaper described the workings of a telephone, back in 1991, BT dismissed the report, saying:

> 'That's how telephones worked a hundred years ago, not now'. [15]

Yet the information used by the paper had been based on BT's own Telecom Technology Showcase exhibition in the City of London.

Then the journalist took a modern, in fact a new, telephone, and cut it open. Did it have the new technology? It did not. So the writer, Neil Johannson, wanted to find out what was going on. Even that was difficult: 'It took me several weeks of pestering to find the right person inside BT who really knows what goes on inside a telephone.' And what was the answer to his question? Nobody knew.

As for the greater movement towards more information, this, in England, provides the same sort of uneasiness and unfamiliarity as the tales from Russia about people trying, ludicrously, to become capitalists. It reminds one of tales of former communists wanting to break down a grandfather clock into wrist-watches.

On the so-called Gatwick Express nearing London, we heard the new-style 'explain it to the customers' announcement of the driver. He apologised for the train's slowness — it was travelling, this Express, at about 20 miles per hour. Then the train stopped dead for some considerable time. Obviously grappling with the horrible need to provide some explanation, he said: 'Apologies for the delay. We are still looking for a platform at Victoria Station.'

A day later, talking to a bossy official on the telephone, I was delighted to hear the unaccustomed words; 'I am sorry'. But he undermined the effect by adding: 'If you won't listen to my apology, I'll come right over and dot you one!'

People do and say things in Britain which foreigners find so inconceivable they have to attribute them to *something*, though nobody knows exactly what. They assume the Brits *must* be deeper than they seem: if only because they so constantly attack each other for being dull. Take this priceless example of – misdirection it must be – from *The Daily Mail,* written by Michael Bywater:

> The anorak perfectly expresses the [British] national character. It discloses (without having to reveal) that underneath the padded, shapeless exterior, there lies a padded, shapeless, quintessentially British body.[16]

Well, that's the body. But why do I insist that there is something else, something in the mind, as well? *The Independent* actually lets it out:

> HOW TO READ BETWEEN THE ENGLISH LINES
> Duplicity is so embedded in the British way of life that foreigners could perhaps be forgiven for getting hold of the wrong end of the stick about the acceptability of untruth.[17]

But, trust the British to be subtler than the foreigner would suspect:

> The deception which is freely practised is the sort which is designed to avoid unkindness.

In the best scientific tradition, one can search for a pattern in examples taken from life. For instance, this deeply mysterious item:

> RAM RAIDERS STOLE CAR WITH NO ENGINE
> Ram raiders who stole a car with no engine had to push it up a hill before they could use it to smash through a shop window.
>   They ignored all the other cars at mechanic Val Quiterio's garage in Plymouth and took a Peugeot which he had been working on. [He said] 'I bought this car from a fisherman who carried crabs in it and it absolutely stinks.'[18]

Cars are a rich source of strange events in Britain. Some years ago, *The Autocar* reported a story about the television personality Raymond Baxter. His car caught fire one evening on the road. A passing motorist stopped while the car was still in flames – and asked him for his autograph.[19]

I pointed out this item to an English friend, who

immediately said, 'There was nothing surprising about a car bursting into flames on an English road: it happens all the time. But you don't see Baxter all the time, except on the telly. That's why you might want his autograph.'

So, perhaps behaviour that seems mystifying could have a possible explanation. However, if anybody doubts that secrecy is endemic in Britain, *The Observer* published a list of things that were officially secret in the mid-nineties:

- Second World War police dental treatment
- Liquor licences for Regents Canal dock workers
- Prince Michael of Kent's training in the RAF
- Visit to Argentina of the Duke of Edinburgh, 1962
- Dangerous driving conditions on a London hump-backed bridge
- The problem of taxi-drivers failing to depress their flags.[20]

Where does all this secrecy get the British? That's probably a secret: I certainly haven't been able to find out. But some things are undoubtedly kept secret too long. The Science Correspondent of *The Daily Telegraph* revealed[21] that something of the sort has happened to Hotol. This, as you are bound to know, is the amazing British space-plane. It is more efficient than anything else of its kind. Unfortunately, two things happened: or, rather, one happened and the other didn't.

What happened was that a brilliant American designer 'read brochures about Hotol, and found it quite easy to work the ideas backwards'. What didn't happen was any *British* development work on the project.

The British themselves always claim that their inertia is inexplicable: but when secrecy is allied to inertia we get what Hotol's inventor, Mr. Alan Bond, called 'a classic example of how Britain forges ahead and then chucks it away without even trying.'

Inventiveness, strange happenings and secrecy, what does it all mean? It all has the feeling of something very old, going back far into the past.

If you start to look into the matter, as a certain American journalist did, you begin to see that all this hidey-hole business has a long, if not wholly respectable, ancestry.

Edmond Taylor, of the *Chicago Tribune*, published his *Awakening from History*[22] in London in 1971. He worked with the Political Warfare Executive in England during World War II. 'I found,' he says, 'the "black" propaganda that they were engaged in producing, and even many of the British "white" programmes, more imaginative and frequently more ruthless than any Nazi psychological warfare I had studied.' He continues:

> The atmosphere of creative nightmare in which my PWE friends lived; the romantic isolation of their country retreat behind its invisible walls of secrecy . . . tended to lure one's rational mind along a labyrinthine way back to a world where magic, white or black, became the true causality . . . I could not help asking myself certain questions. One, which I wondered about quite a bit but tactfully refrained from putting to my hosts, concerned the basis of operational doctrine upon which PWE had been so quickly, yet apparently so solidly, built. The agency was strictly a wartime administrative creation but almost everything about it – except, perhaps, the personalities of its staff – bespoke an ancient experience in the techniques of dissension and demoralization. From what secret peacetime drawers had the British taken out all these recipes for exploiting human weakness, all these mental philtres, all these scoundrel skills accumulated through centuries of power struggle in every quarter of the globe, which they were now so generously making available to an upstart ally and potential successor?

Unfortunately for some of us, Mr. Taylor 'never discovered the full answer'. He did, however, determine that there had 'always existed the indispensable foundations for rapid expansion: a pool of trained personnel, a current technology of clandestine operations, and the necessary structure of administrative control.'

Secret meanings, hidden hands, amazing inventiveness – these are the mysterious fascinations of the British. Will anyone ever know why?

Foreword

1) *Darkest England*, Idries Shah (Octagon Press Ltd., London) 1987
2) *The Daily Telegraph*, 16 May 1987
3) *The Daily Telegraph*, 26 November 1991

Chapter 2

1) *The Sunday Times*, September 1988

Chapter 3

1) *The Evening Standard*, London, 14 June 1991
2) *The Independent (History in the Making)*, 28 December 1992

Chapter 5

1) *The Life of Samuel Johnson*, James Boswell (Printed by Henry Baldwin, for Charles Dilly) 1791
2) *The International Herald Tribune*, 14 February 1991
3) *The Times*, 28 January 1991

Chapter 6

1) *England's Heritage?* B.K. Sen, 1987
2) *The Natives are Restless*, Idries Shah (Octagon Press Ltd., London) 1988
3) *The Sunday Telegraph*, 11 February 1993

Chapter 7

1) *The Independent Magazine*, 15 June 1991
2) *General Amin*, David Martin (Faber & Faber) 1974
3) *The Evening Standard*, London, 11 April 1991

Chapter 8

1) *My Years with the Arabs*, General Sir John Glubb (Institute for Cultural Research) 1971
2) *A Course in Spoken Arabic*, Oxford University Press, 1978

Chapter 9

1) *The Sunday Times*, 5 July 1992
2) *The Purloined Letter*, Edgar Allen Poe (*Chambers' Edinburgh Magazine*) 1844
3) *The Independent*, 12 December 1992
4) *The Evening Standard*, London, 17 June 1992

5) *The Sunday Telegraph Magazine*, 4 October 1987
6) *The Observer*, 13 December 1992

Chapter 10
1) *The Life and Times of Lieut.-General Sir James Moncreiffe*,
    D. S. Macdiarmid (Constable & Co.) 1923.
2) *Wanderings in Arabia*, Charles Doughty (Duckworth & Co.) 1908
3) *Travels and Adventures in Egypt, Arabia and Persia,*William Perry
    Fogg (Dustin, Gilman & Co.) 1874

Chapter 11
1) *Kings and Things: First Stories from English History*,
    (Nelson & Sons) 1937
2) *The Times*, 21 November 1988
3) *The Summing Up*, Somerset Maugham (Heinemann & Co.) 1938
4) *The Sunday Times*, 1 June 1986
5) *The Daily Telegraph*, 24 February 1993
6) *The Daily Telegraph*, 23 February 1993
7) *The Evening Standard*, London, 26 May 1990
8) *The Independent*, 2 January 1993
9) *The Observer*, 13 December 1992

Chapter 12
1) *The Times*, 14 March, 1992
2) *Haydn's Dictionary of Dates*, Benjamin Vincent
    (E. Moxon & Sons) 1878
3) *A Dictionary of Common Fallacies*, Peter Ward (Oleander) 1978
4) *Dictionary of Music and Musicians*, ed: George Grove
    (Macmillan) 1940; Vol. I
5) *The Daily Telegraph*, 10 March 1993
6) *Darkest England*, Idries Shah (Octagon Press Ltd., London)
    1987 p. 23
7) *The Daily Telegraph*, 16 April 1992
8) *Those English!* Kurt von Stutterheim (Sidgwick & Jackson)
    1937
9) Quoted in *The Listener*, 6 March 1986
10) *The Times*, 29 August 1981
11) *The Times*, 6 July 1987
12) *The Evening Standard*, London, 19 February 1993
13) *The Sunday Telegraph*, 21 February 1993
14) *The Times*, 23 November 1991

Chapter 13

1) *The Observer*, 14 May 1989
2) *The Sunday Telegraph Magazine*, 17 May 1987
3) *The Daily Telegraph*, Robert Bedlow (Estates Correspondent), 2 November 1986
4) *The Sunday Telegraph*, 20 December 1992
5) *The Times*, 6 July 1991
6) *The Daily Mail*, 29 March 1991
7) *The Management of Science*, Sir Douglas Hague, Editor 1991
8) *The Evening Standard*, London, 3 June 1991
9) *The Observer*, 26 June 1992
10) *The Daily Telegraph*, 23 May 1991
11) *The Observer Magazine*, 20 December 1992
12) *The Times*, 3 December 1992
13) *The Daily Telegraph*, 29 September 1991
14) *The Independent*, 14 February 1993
15) *The Daily Telegraph*, 21 January 1989
16) *The Sunday Telegraph*, 14 May 1989

Chapter 14

1) *The Times*, 17 June 1992
2) *The Times*, 16 June 1992
3) *The Daily Mail*, 21 May 1992
4) *The Sunday Telegraph*, 28 May 1989
5) *The Daily Mail*, 15 March 1993
6) *The Daily Telegraph*, 18 July 1991
7) Quoted in *The Independent*, 4 March 1993
8) *The Times*, 10 June 1991
9) *The Observer*, 5 July 1992
10) *The Independent*, 10 June 1991
11) *The Telegraph*, 3 June 1991
12) *The Independent*, 23 February 1992
13) *New Society*, 3 July 1987
14) *The Times*, 5 June 1991
15) *The Times*, 5 January 1991
16) Quoted by Maureen Cleave in *The Evening Standard*, London, 22 May 1987
17) *The Times*, 20 May 1989
18) *The Mail on Sunday*, 28 June 1987
19) *The Evening Standard*, London, 12 July 1991

Chapter 15

1) From Ms. Eileen Kilpatrick, 12 September 1988
2) *The Daily Telegraph*, 29 October 1992
3) *The Daily Telegraph*, 11 January 1993
4) *The Daily Mail*, 27 May 1991
5) *The Daily Mail*, 27 March 1992
6) *The Daily Telegraph*, 3 January 1993
7) Issued on 17 December 1992
8) *The Evening Standard*, London, 8 April 1992
9) *The Daily Telegraph*, 4 December 1991
10) *The Independent*, 27 July 1991
11) *The Daily Telegraph*, 13 May 1989
12) *The Times*, 28 December 1992
13) *The Daily Telegraph*, 24 March 1991
14) *The Sunday Telegraph*, 24 January 1993
15) *The Observer*, 14 February 1993
16) *The British Medical Journal*, 22 December 1990
17) *The Daily Telegraph*, 17 February 1993
18) *The Daily Telegraph*, 3 February 1993
19) *The Times*, 3 December 1992

Chapter 16

1) *Daily Express*, 15 March 1956
2) *The Times*, 4 May 1992
3) *The Daily Telegraph*, 4 May 1985
4) *The Independent*, 6 July 1987
5) *The Times*, 22 September 1992
6) *The Evening Standard*, London, 9 April 1992
7) *The Mail on Sunday*, 3 May 1992
8) *The Daily Telegraph*, 21 September 1988
9) *The Evening Standard*, London, 9 March 1990
10) *A Sparrow's Flight*, Lord Hailsham of St. Marylebone (William Collins & Son) 1990
11) *The Times*, 15 January 1993
12) *The Independent*, 30 January 1993
13) *The Times*, 13 June 1992
14) *The Daily Telegraph*, 21 June 1991

Chapter 17

1) *The Daily Telegraph*, 24 December 1992
2) *The Daily Telegraph*, 10 June 1991
3) *The Daily Telegraph*, 9 September 1991
4) *The Daily Telegraph*, 12 February 1993
5) *The Listener*, 30 May 1985
6) *The Daily Telegraph*, 20 February 1993

Chapter 18

1) *The Independent*, 5 October 1987
2) *The Institute for Health Sciences Journal*, Winter 92/3
3) Commons Public Accounts Committee Report, 17 May 1991

Chapter 19

1) *The Times*, 19 May 1992
2) *The Daily Telegraph*, 27 June 1992
3) *Kara Kush*, Idries Shah (William Collins & Son) 1986
4) *The Independent*, 20 August 1992
5) *The Telegraph*, 6 March 1993
6) *Super-Scrooge*, Malcolm Stacey (Quiller Press) 1991
7) *The Times*, 26 December 1992

Chapter 20

1) *The Sunday Times*, 30 April 1989
2) *Recollections and Reflections*, Sir Thomas Fraser (Blackwood) 1914
3) *Trackers and Smugglers in the Deserts of Egypt*, Colonel André von Dumreicher (Methuen) 1931
4) *Letters from the East*, John Carne (Colburn & Bentley, London) 1830
5) *Wanderings in Arabia*, Charles Doughty (Duckworth & Co.) 1908
6) *The Arab of the Desert*, H.R.P. Dickson (Allen & Unwin) 1949
7) *The Rich Man's Guide to Europe*, Charles Graves (Prentice-Hall) 1966
8) *Wanderings and Wonderings*, John Aubertin (Keegan, Paul & Co, London) 1892
9) *Many Memories*, J.H. Rivett-Carnac (Blackwood) 1910
10) *The Independent Magazine*, 4 March 1989
11) *The Independent*, 12 January 1993
12) *The Evening Standard*, London, 19 July 1970
13) *The Independent Book Review*, 17 February 1989

Chapter 21
1) *The Evening Standard*, London, 5 January 1993

Chapter 22
1) *The Independent*, 7 January 1991
2) *The English People,* D.W. Brogan (Hamish Hamilton) 1944
3) Quoted in *The Guardian* 2 December 1992

Chapter 23
1) *The Mail on Sunday*, 3 January 1993
2) *The Times*, 16 May 1987
3) *The Daily Mail Magazine*, 4 March 1989
4) *The Mail on Sunday*, 16 August 1987
5) *The Independent*, 11 August 1987
6) *The Times*, 12 July 1991
7) *The Evening Standard*, London, 16 March 1992
8) *The Daily Telegraph*, 15 September 1987
9) *The Daily Telegraph*, 10 June 1991
10) *The Times*, 6 July 1991
11) *The Daily Telegraph*, 5 March 1992
12) Summarised by Jonathan Petrie in *The Daily Telegraph*, 25 November 1992
13) *The Daily Telegraph*, 6 May 1989
14) *The Independent Magazine*, 12 August 1989
15) Penelope Stokes, 3 March, 1988

Chapter 24
1) *The Times*, 2 March 1993
2) *The Independent on Sunday*, 28 February 1993
3) *The Daily Telegraph*, 22 February 1993
4) *The Independent on Sunday*, 30 September 1990
5) *The Observer*, 30 June 1991
6) *The Daily Telegraph*, 12 December 1992
7) *The Independent on Sunday*, 30 September 1990
8) *The Independent*, 28 November 1992
9) *The Daily Telegraph*, 23 March 1992
10) *The Evening Standard*, London, 25 April 1991
11) *The Daily Telegraph*, 24 March 1991
12) *The Daily Telegraph*, 23 September 1991
13) *The Independent*, 25 November 1991

14) *The Times*, 20 January 1993
15) *The Times*, 25 August 1987
16) *The Times*, 5 March 1993

Chapter 25
1) *The Guardian*, 18 February 1993
2) *The Times*, 28 August 1987
3) *The Natives Are Restless*, Idries Shah (Octagon Press Ltd., London) 1988
4) *The Sunday Telegraph*, 24 January 1993
5) *Battle for the Mind*, Dr William Sargant (William Heinemann Ltd.) 1957
6) *Oriental Magic*, Idries Shah (Octagon Press Ltd., London) 1956, 1992
7) *The Secret Lore Of Magic*, Idries Shah (Frederick Muller) 1957
8) *The Sufis*, Idries Shah (Octagon Press Ltd., London) 1964, 1977
9) *The Way of the Sufi*, Idries Shah (Octagon Press Ltd., London) 1968, 1980
10) *The Times*, 18 September 1991
11) *The Daily Mail*, 5 November 1988
12) *The Daily Telegraph*, 3 July 1992
13) *The Times*, 13 May 1986
14) *The Sunday Times*, 1 January 1992
15) Reported in *The New Scientist*, 8 June 1991
16) *Daily Mail*, 27 May 1989
17) *The Independent*, 21 March 1990
18) *The Evening Standard*, London, 3 December 1992
19) *Autocar*, 6 March 1985
20) *The Observer*, 21 February 1993
21) *The Daily Telegraph*, 21 January 1989
22) *Awakening From History*, Edmond Taylor (Chatto & Windus) 1971

For More Information about Sufism,
and to be on our mailing list, write:
The Society for Sufi Studies
P.O. Box 43
Los Altos, CA 94023
or go to the web at http://www.sufis.org